EDUCATION

OF THE

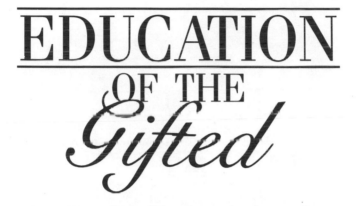

Gifted

PROGRAMS AND PERSPECTIVES

by Joan Franklin Smutny
and
Rita Haynes Blocksom

A Publication of the Phi Delta Kappa Educational Foundation
Bloomington, Indiana

Cover design by Victoria Voelker

Library of Congress Catalog Card Number 89-62396
ISBN 0-87367-445-6

This monograph is sponsored by the District Representative and Area Coordinators of Phi Delta Kappa District VI, who made a generous contribution toward publication costs. They sponsor this monograph to honor the memory of their friend and colleague, the late Joseph E. Nove, who served as Area 6L Coordinator.

Joseph E. Nove was a loyal Kappan, caring educator, and a loving and devoted husband and father. He was deeply committed to serving the young, to educational excellence, and to the Phi Delta Kappa ideals of Leadership, Research, and Service. He will always be remembered for his warmth and understanding and for the wise counsel he provided in carrying out the goals of Phi Delta Kappa.

James V. Fogarty, District VI Representative

District VI Area Coordinators:

George W. Crane
Michael J. Dorgan
Eugene L. Hammer
Arnold E. Kelley
Wayne R. King
Joel R. Oppenheim
Stephen A. Pavlak

Ronald L. Peterson
Luther W. Pfluger
John M. Skalski
Charles F. Smith
Karol Strelecki
Evelyn P. Valentine
William J. Vaugh
Barry J. Wilson

ACKNOWLEDGMENTS

We would like to acknowledge several educators and scholars in gifted education who have influenced the thinking reflected in these pages. They include Paul Torrance, Dorothy Sisk, June Cox, Barbara Clark, Margie Kitano, Calvin Taylor, Judy Eby, Frank Williams, Benjamin Bloom, James T. Webb, and Joseph Renzulli, who wrote the foreword. We also acknowledge the support provided by staff of the National College of Education's Center for Gifted. They are Cheryl Siewers and Erin Wiggins. Finally, we wish to thank Derek L. Burleson, Editor of Special Publications at Phi Delta Kappa, for his perceptive editing.

FOREWORD

Special programs for gifted and talented students have been neglected too long in our nation's schools. However, the climate has changed radically in recent years, and we are at last enjoying a "renaissance" of interest in making appropriate provisions for our most able learners. Undoubtedly, a good deal of the motivation for reassessing the need for special programming for the gifted resulted from several reform reports of the early 1980s, notably *A Nation at Risk*, which pointed out that "our once unchallenged preeminence in commerce, industry, science, and technological innovation is being overtaken by competitors throughout the world . . . if an unfriendly foreign power had attempted to impose on America the mediocre educational performance that exists today, we might well have viewed it as an act of war."

These kinds of concerns have caused national policy makers to realize that gifted and talented young people are the most precious national resource a country can have. It is from this group of high potential youth that a civilization derives contributions in the arts and sciences, health care, agriculture, manufacturing, transportation, and many other areas that collectively represent the advancement of a society. Special opportunities for high potential youth are not a "luxury item" for our education system, but rather the very essence of what it takes to stimulate the growth and creative development of a civilization.

The renewed interest in providing programs for highly able children and youth has resulted in many new and exciting developments in the field of gifted and talented education. Many new research studies have been undertaken and reported in journals devoted to giftedness and creativity. Membership in professional organizations serving the gifted and talented has increased dramatically over the past decade. And each year school districts throughout the nation report that they are earmarking more and more teaching positions for the gifted and talented.

With the growth in all aspects of programming for the gifted and talented has come a need for information by teachers and administrators who are attempting to implement new services or to modify existing programs. The authors of this book provide both an introduction and an overall perspective on most of the topics related to sound program development for the gifted. The book covers current topics, issues, and concerns of interest to persons working with high ability children and youth. The authors draw on their extensive backgrounds and many years of experience in teaching and program development in gifted education, and they have provided extensive references for persons interested in pursuing several topics in greater depth. The authors also have punctuated their text with several sample teaching activities and curricular materials, which should prove helpful to those who need to see programming ideas translated into actual practice. Thus, this book can serve as an introductory text, a program development guide, or a general resource in the field of education of the gifted.

Readers will find this book practical, easy to read, and filled with the kind of wisdom that only persons who have spent many years teaching and supervising gifted education can offer. In a highly readable style, the authors present information that draws on many theories, points of view, and existing program structures on gifted education. Although there is a vast amount of literature on gifted education, the authors have carefully selected and organized the kinds of resources that will be of most help to educators when dealing with the tremendous responsibilities and challenges in gifted education in the decade ahead.

Joseph S. Renzulli
University of Connecticut

TABLE OF CONTENTS

CHAPTER ONE
Identification of the Gifted

Identifying giftedness is no simple task. History is replete with examples of gifted individuals who were overlooked in childhood. Sir Isaac Newton was a failure throughout much of his school career and considered to be an idle tinkerer until he formulated the Laws of Gravity. Caruso's parents wanted him to be an engineer, and his music teacher said he had no voice at all. Louis Pasteur, Louisa May Alcott, Walt Disney, F.W. Woolworth, and Charles Darwin were told they would never succeed in their chosen fields. These people received no recognition during their school years, nor were they provided with special programs or accelerated content.

In 1972, Sidney Marland, then U.S. Commissioner of Education, prepared a definition of giftedness to serve as a guideline for the federal programs for the gifted being initiated at that time. It has been widely quoted:

> Gifted and talented children are those, identified by professional and qualified persons, who by virtue of outstanding abilities are capable of high performance. These are children who require differentiated educational programs and/or services beyond those normally provided by the regular school program in order to realize their contributions to self and society.
>
> Children capable of high performance include those with demonstrated achievement or potential in the following categories, singly or in combination:
>
> 1. General intellectual ability (with I.Q. scores in the top 3-5%)
> 2. Specific academic ability
> 3. Creative and productive thinking
> 4. Leadership ability
> 5. Visual and performing arts
> 6. Psychomotor ability*

---

*This category was dropped from the definition of giftedness under the Gifted and Talented Children's Education Act of 1978 (Marland 1972).

Barbara Clark (1988) states that giftedness may be related to biological differences in the brain:

> It is now possible to speak of the gifted as having at least three areas of advanced or increased brain growth. . . . Such brain development may partially manifest itself in outstanding cognitive ability, academic aptitude, creative behavior, leadership ability or ability in visual and performing arts. How giftedness will be expressed depends on the genetic patterns and anatomical structure of the individual and the support and the opportunities by the individual's environment. (pp. 6-7)

Thus, according to Clark, the innate qualities of giftedness can be fully realized or remain undeveloped depending on environmental opportunities. Gifted education is essentially one of providing those environmental opportunities. Ideally, each child should be tested individually and given a wide range of opportunities to demonstrate talent. In practice, insufficient resources prevent this kind of extensive professional testing. However, there is a middle ground. Barbara Clark (1988) offers a multi-dimensional screening process to identify those children most likely to be gifted, thus narrowing down the candidates to a manageable pool for individual testing. She also offers other assessment procedures for those areas of giftedness, such as leadership and visual and performing arts, that are not readily identified through traditional testing methods.

Screening

Barbara Clark recommends seven screening approaches: 1) nominations from teacher, principal, psychologist, parent, peers, or self; 2) teacher reports on student's intellectual, physical, social, and emotional functioning, as well as learning style and motivation; 3) family history and student background as provided by parents including early development and the student's out-of-school activities and interests; 4) peer identification; 5) student inventory of interests; 6) student work and achievement; and 7) a variety of tests including group achievement and group intelligence (p. 222).

Clark's multi-dimensional approach seeks to minimize false-positives, (children who appear gifted but are not) or false-negatives (failing to identify children who are gifted). Given the limitations of current identification procedures, Swassing (1985) stresses that it is better to over-identify than under-identify, thus minimizing the chances of children being overlooked.

Clark notes a number of pitfalls in relying solely on teachers for screening. Teachers tend to identify those children who excel in those areas in which the teacher excels or who conform to the rules of the classroom. Even the highly gifted are not always readily identified by teachers; however, teachers can become better identifiers of the gifted by providing them with a list of behavioral characteristics. A number of these lists have been published (see Clark 1988; Swassing 1985; and Eby and Smutny 1990).

Although the stereotype of gifted children is one of a model student, they can, in fact, exhibit characteristics that teachers find quite irritating. Swassing offers several examples of such behavior. They may: dominate discussions; resist rules, regulations, and standardized procedures; use humor to manipulate; and lose interest quickly. Sometimes when gifted children exhibit these behaviors, they can be mislabeled as hyperactive or dubbed the "class clown." So, although behavioral checklists can be helpful in screening, they may not always be reliable.

Identification Procedures

Panel members for the National Report on Identification: Assessment and Recommendations for Comprehensive Identification of Gifted and Talented Youth (Richert 1985) recommend six principles to observe when establishing identification procedures for the gifted:

1. Advocacy. Identification should be designed in the best interests of all students.
2. Defensibility. Procedures should be based on the best available research and recommendations.
3. Equity. Procedures should guarantee that no one is overlooked. The civil rights of students should be protected. Strategies should be outlined for identifying the disadvantaged gifted.
4. Pluralism. The broadest defensible definition of giftedness should be used.
5. Comprehensiveness. As many gifted learners as possible should be identified and served.
6. Pragmatism. Whenever possible, procedures should allow for the modification and use of tools and resources on hand (pp. 68-69).

Use of Testing

A number of intelligence tests are available for assessing cognitive abilities, including the Revised Stanford-Binet Test of Intelligence, the Wechsler Intelligence Scales for Children-Revised, the Cognitive Abilities Test, the Differential Aptitude Tests, and the Kaufman Assessment Battery for Children (K-ABC). Achievement tests are commonly used. Tests of creativity also are useful instruments, for example, the Williams Test of Creativity or the Torrance Test of Creative Thinking.

When intelligence or achievement tests are used to identify gifted students, their scores usually fall in the top 3% to 5% of the population, with an I.Q. of 130 generally used as a cut-off point for admission to gifted programs. However, this can vary widely in school systems across the country, with cut-off scores ranging from 120 to 140. Highly gifted people, often labeled geniuses, have I.Q.s of 160 and up.

The use of I.Q. and achievement tests as the sole or major means of identifying gifted students has come under much criticism. Susan Richert (1985) notes five common abuses of tests for identification purposes:

> 1. Educational equity is being violated in the identification of significant sub-populations. In national figures published by the U.S. Department of Education's Office of Civil Rights, minority groups such as Blacks, Hispanics and Native Americans are under-represented by 30-70% in gifted programs. These figures are collected each year, but are evidently considered so controversial that they have not been published since 1980.
> 2. Identification instruments are being used to identify categories of giftedness for which they are not designed. For example, I.Q. and achievement tests are used almost interchangeably and to identify areas of giftedness such as leadership and creativity.
> 3. Instruments and procedures are being used at inappropriate stages of identification. The use of diagnostic tests is common.
> 4. Multiple criteria are being combined inappropriately. For example, I.Q. scores, scores from a creativity test, and checklist nomination forms are all weighed and scored to produce one number for the child; then selection is based on that number.
> 5. Some gifted students are consistently screened out by present practices. Most identification criteria focus on selecting academic achievers based on measurements that are limited to achievement tests, I.Q. tests, grades, and teacher recommendations. (pp. 69-70)

Another criticism leveled at using testing for selecting students for gifted programs is that the test may not be content-related to the program. What is the point of using composite achievement test scores for selecting students for a gifted mathematics program?

According to Richert, the use of multiple identification criteria that draw on both formal and informal procedures over a longer assessment period would help to break down the authority of a single score and establish a sounder basis for identifying talent in many neglected sub-populations.

In selecting tests, Swassing (1985) offers the following guiding questions: Are the tests valid for the group to be tested? Do the tests measure achievement or intelligence? Are the tests reliable? How do the achievement tests reflect the goals of the program in which the selected students will be placed? Can we interpret the results of the testing in terms of the statistical properties of the test?

Robert Sternberg has much to say about testing and identification of giftedness. A proponent of multiple intelligences, he defines three types: contextual, experiential, and internal. Contextual intelligence refers to adapting to the environment; experiential intelligence builds on past experiences for solving new problems; internal intelligence is used to approach problems, evaluate feedback, and make decisions about the appropriate approach to the problem. Sternberg's theories are developed more fully in *Beyond I.Q.: A Triarchic Theory of Human Intelligence* (1984).

Sternberg (1982) maintains that abilities and behaviors necessary for successful test-taking are often the opposite of gifted behaviors and argues that four "dubious assumptions" underlie our use of the standardized test:

1. To be smart is to be fast.
2. Intelligence is last year's achievement. "Virtually all tests commonly used for the assessment of intelligence place heavy achievement demand on the students tested" (p. 158). This is particularly discriminatory against children outside the normal sociocultural milieu.
3. Testing needs to be conducted in a stressful, anxiety-provoking situation.
4. Precision is tantamount to validity. People are impressed by the exactness of numbers, associating numbers with accuracy without questioning the validity of how the numbers were obtained.

Sternberg does not advocate total disregard for I.Q. and achievement testing but warns that for certain individuals it is not a valid indicator of giftedness.

Howard Gardner, in *Frames of Mind: The Theory of Multiple Intelligences* (1983), postulates seven intelligences that are found in most people but differ in their level of development. In Gardner's framework, intelligence is defined as a set of skills that enable an individual to define and solve problems. Gardner's seven intelligences are:

1. Linguistic intelligence: oral and auditory abilities as evidenced in oral and written expression.
2. Logical intelligence: mathematical reasoning and the ability to "handle skillfully long chains of reasoning" (p. 139).
3. Spatial intelligence: visual/spatial acumen as evidenced in artistic and scientific contributions.
4. Musical intelligence: auditory ability resulting in composition and musical performance.

5. Kinesthetic intelligence: physical ability resulting in prowess in athletics or dance.
6. Intrapersonal intelligence: inner qualities resulting in a high degree of self-knowledge and understanding.
7. Interpersonal intelligence: qualities reflected in leadership and empathy for others.

Individuals may have exceptional abilities in any one of Gardner's intelligences or in a combination of them. Thus, giftedness may find expression in a great range of abilities that a single I.Q. score could not possibly communicate; and Gardner's theory accounts for the great diversity of talent found among those with the same I.Q. score.

Joseph Renzulli offers still a different approach to identifying the gifted. In his model, giftedness involves three overlapping areas: above-average ability, high levels of task commitment, and high levels of creativity, represented by three interlocking circles. Giftedness occurs when those three circles overlap substantially. Stated another way, superior ability alone is not sufficient; there also must be motivation and creative expression. His approach challenges the assumption that giftedness is innate in an elite group of people and that those who are born gifted are gifted for a lifetime. Renzulli is also critical of using only testing to identify the gifted, arguing that individuals so identified tend to be those with well-developed test-taking skills (Renzulli, Reis, and Smith 1981).

Renzulli's model of gifted education uses the metaphor of a revolving-door that allows students to move in and out of special programs depending on their needs and interests. The model requires a talent pool of one-quarter to one-third of the school population. These students are allowed to pursue in-depth research on a topic until their interest is satisfied. At that time, they move out of the gifted program. Using this model better serves the interests, abilities, and learning style of the individual student. A student may be cycled back into the program when another project of interest arises. "In a sense, the revolving-door approach means that a child 'earns' the opportunity to obtain special services by showing some or all of those traits research has associated with giftedness: above-average ability, task commitment, and creativity" (p. 649).

Research by Renzulli and Reis validates the revolving-door model. For two control groups, those who scored in the top 5% on standardized tests and those with above-average abilities but who scored less than in the top 5%, there were no significant differences with the two groups in respect to the quality of students' products (Reis and Renzulli 1982, p. 620).

Gifted Behaviors

Some educators argue that there are no gifted children, only gifted behaviors. Judy Eby (1983) notes the paradox that "children who are selected (for gifted programs) on the basis of test scores are not always the same children who are at the head of their classes, asking for harder, more challenging work" (p. 32). This prompted her to develop an identification method emphasizing gifted behaviors. Based on Renzulli's model, she offers a general selection matrix and teacher recommendation form that systematically evaluates test scores and gifted behaviors more equitably. Eby stresses that the elitist stigma associated with labeling children as "gifted" can be side-stepped by focusing identification on behaviors. "Gifted behavior . . . is not confined to a selected few . . . gifted behavior is displayed when a child uses and follows through to the completion of a task. It may appear at any time, in any child, and may disappear or reappear periodically according to the child's need for challenge and accomplishment" (p. 33).

Even with these expanded views of intelligence and various approaches to identifying giftedness, many children may still be overlooked. Too often the means of identification only mirror current societal values and existing programming. An excerpt from Paul Torrance's (1985) article "Who Is Gifted?" illustrates this point:

> John Torres was a strong, energetic, 12-year-old sixth-grader who had never learned to read. He was known as the school's vandal. Although no one could ever prove that he and the boys he led made a shambles of the school each weekend, he had been a problem for teachers almost from the first day of his schooling. No one thought he could learn. His sixth-grade teacher thought he was gifted. He was a veritable mechanical genius and could repair any kind of audio-visual equipment or anything else mechanical. He was also a genius in leadership. He could attract other boys, organize them, and lead them in doing almost anything. His artwork was also superior. His teacher started by getting the student council to appoint him as head of the lunchroom committee to help arrange the school cafeteria and keep things functioning. He recruited other boys to help and this was the beginning of many other leadership activities for him in improving the school. The vandalism in the school ceased. John learned to read about as well as almost any other sixth-grader and loved to go to school. Was John Torres gifted? Would it be better to treat John as gifted in the psychomotor and leadership areas or as a retarded non-reader and a behavior disorder case? Which is in John's best interest? Which is in society's best interest? (p. 2)

Conclusion

The research on the nature of intelligence and the diverse definitions of giftedness require that we broaden the selection criteria for gifted programs, using a multi-dimensional approach that includes parent, teacher, and self nomination as well as intelligence, achievement, and creativity tests. One test score from one kind of test can no longer be considered a balanced or fair means of identification. Also, the evidence that I.Q. and achievement tests are culturally biased and that, to some extent, test-wiseness accounts for higher scores cannot be ignored.

Whether giftedness is innate or represents certain behavioral characteristics is also a matter of conflicting opinion. Teachers have long known that children with high I.Q.s do not necessarily evidence high task commitment. Is it appropriate to leave them out of gifted programming? Is it appropriate to exclude high achievers who do not meet I.Q. requirements? The resolution of these issues calls for a balanced approach.

Moreover, a multi-definition of giftedness becomes a moot point if gifted programming remains focused only on academic achievers. What is the point of identifying a child as talented in the arts if there are no arts programs? Should that child's untapped talents go unrecognized any more than the mathematically precocious? As the concept of giftedness broadens, so must gifted programming diversify.

References

Clark, B. *Growing Up Gifted*. 3rd ed. Columbus, Ohio: Charles E. Merrill, 1988.

Eby, J.W. "Gifted Behavior: A Developmental Approach." *Illinois Council for the Gifted Journal* 4 (1985): 7-9.

Eby, J.W. "Gifted Behavior: A Non-Elitist Approach." *Educational Leadership* (May 1983): 30-36.

Eby, J.W., and Smutny, J.F. *A Thoughtful Overview of Gifted Education*. White Plains, N.Y.: Longman, 1990.

Ehrlich, V. *Gifted Children: A Guide for Parents and Teachers*. New York: Trillium Press, 1985.

Gallagher, J. *Teaching the Gifted Child*. Boston: Allyn & Bacon, 1985.

Gardner, H. *Frames of Mind: The Theory of Multiple Intelligences*. New York: Basic Books, 1983.

Marland, S., Jr. *Education of the Gifted and Talented*. Report to the Congress of the United States by the U.S. Commissioner of Education. Washington, D.C.: U.S. Government Printing Office, 1972.

Reis, S.M., and Renzulli, J.S. "A Case for a Broadened Conception of Giftedness." *Phi Delta Kappan* 63 (May 1982): 619-20.

Renzulli, J.S.; Reis, S.M.; and Smith, L.H. "The Revolving-Door Model: A New Way of Identifying the Gifted." *Phi Delta Kappan* 62 (May 1981): 648-49.

Richert, E.S. "Identification of Gifted Students: An Update." *Roeper Review*, 8 (November 1985): 68-72.

Shaw, F.W., II. "Identification of the Gifted: Design Defects and the Law." *Urban Education* 21, no. 1 (1986): 42-61.

Sternberg, R. *Beyond I.Q.: A Triarachic Theory of Human Intelligence*. New Rochelle, N.Y.: Cambridge University Press, 1984.

Sternberg, R. "Lies We Live By: Misapplication of Tests in Identifying the Gifted." *Gifted Child Quarterly* 26 (1982): 157-61.

Swassing, R.H. *Teaching Gifted Children and Adolescents*. Columbus, Ohio: Charles E. Merrill, 1985.

Torrance, Paul. "Who Is Gifted?" *Illinois Council for the Gifted Journal* 4 (1985): 2-3.

Treffinger, D.J., and Renzulli, J.S. "Giftedness as Potential for Creative Productivity: Transcending I.Q. Scores." *Roeper Review* 7, No. 3 (1986): 150-54.

U.S. Congress. *Education Act of 1978*. Washington, D.C.: U.S. Government Printing Office, 1978.

CHAPTER TWO
Strategies for
Teaching the Gifted

"What do you know that's invisible?" asked the teacher at a Saturday morning program for gifted four-year-olds in a suburb of Chicago. "Ghosts," "love," "the wind," were some of the replies from the eager youngsters, who were learning about air. Asking open-ended questions produces creative answers even from preschoolers.

After sketching the basic properties of air to the preschoolers, the teacher asked: "How can you put a paper napkin in water without getting it wet?" The teacher then stuffed a napkin in the bottom of a glass, inverted the glass, and placed it in a bowl of water. She then withdrew the glass and pulled out the dry napkin, thus demonstrating that air kept the water from touching the napkin. Other science activities involving air included picking up a paper cup without touching it with your hands (by sucking on a hole in the bottom), and inflating a balloon without blowing into it (by putting it over the lip of a bottle and placing the bottle over a lighted candle).

Down the hall, a group of gifted preschoolers was playing a traffic game inside a miniature city they had built with blocks. Another group was exploring visual images in a creative movement class. The primary-level gifted science class was experimenting with a balloon, a string, and weights to explore the concepts of weight and mass.

Such activities illustrate how direct involvement and hands-on activities can help young children learn complex concepts and apply them to other situations. These children are learning by manipulating familiar materials, analyzing what happens, and then coming up with innovative solutions to unfamiliar problems.

In the process of working through experiments creatively, children become active thinkers rather than just consumers of information. By allowing children to approach the curriculum through problem solving, experimentation, and invention, they learn to apply these skills to problems beyond the confines of school. E. Paul Torrance, a pioneer in gifted education, saw the need to make creative and critical thinking a priority for the schools. In a 1960 speech at the Education for the Space Age Conference, he said:

> One of the most revolutionary changes I foresee is a revision of the objectives of education. Today we proclaim that our schools exist for learning. We say that we must get tougher and make pupils learn more. Schools of the future will be designed not only for learning, but also for thinking. More and more insistently, today's schools and colleges are being asked to produce men and women who can think, who can find adequate solutions to impelling world problems, who cannot be brainwashed, men and women who can adapt to change and maintain sanity in this age of acceleration.

With the current emphasis on teaching thinking, perhaps Torrance's vision of the school of the future can become reality. As reported in *Developing Minds: A Resource Book for Teaching Thinking* (Costa 1985), the focus of instruction is on the development of strategies and techniques that teach the process of thinking rather than the products of knowledge. For the gifted this focus becomes an essential element of the curriculum.

Although teaching thinking is an important component of gifted programs, Torrance's research suggests that thinking and creativity are not separate entities. Rather, they go hand in hand, because creativity functions directly in the critical thinking process. In teaching the gifted, we must address both critical and creative thinking. Gifted children learn both processes concurrently. Let's briefly review the meanings of critical and creative thinking and see how they function in the gifted education program.

Critical and Creative Thinking in the Classroom

Critical thinking involves analysis, synthesis, and evaluation. Benjamin Bloom, in *The Taxonomy of Educational Objectives: The Classification of Educational Goals* (1956), has organized cognitive functions into six levels. Familiarity with these six levels is useful for teachers of the gifted when planning learning activities that promote higher cognitive functioning. The six levels of Bloom's taxonomy are as follows:

1. Knowledge: At this level students are able to recall basic facts, give definitions, and provide descriptions. This level is most commonly associated with rote learning and drill. Knowledge requires recognition, identification, listing, naming, or locating. Through questions and answers teachers can determine whether basic facts have been learned.

2. Comprehension: Students are able to summarize or provide examples that explain their understanding of a concept or principle.

11

3. Application: At this level students are able to illustrate, construct, or apply principles to solve a wide range of problems in any subject area.

4. Analysis: At this level learners interrelate knowledge and concepts in abstract terms. Students may classify, compare, contrast, investigate, or deduce. Experiments in science, small-group discussions in social studies, and expository writing in language arts are examples of activities where students operate at the analysis level. Analysis skills are triggered by such questions as: How does the invention of the laser beam compare to the invention of the computer? What factors led to the Civil War? What principles of art are demonstrated in a Monet painting? The analytical process involved in answering such questions often leads to creative thinking, for example, writing a scenario of what would have happened if the South had won the Civil War.

5. Synthesis: While analysis dissects knowledge, synthesis arranges and rearranges knowledge and ideas to create an original piece of work. Examples of synthesis include writing a story, giving a speech, or developing a theory to explain why one kind of soil is better for growing peanuts. It can be as simple as retelling a story with a new and different ending or as complex as developing a hypothesis to explain why several historical events occurred or why several science experiments failed. Students compose, invent, design, write, produce, plan, and develop at the synthesis level.

6. Evaluation: This level is the most complex and requires the highest order of thinking. At this level students use accepted criteria to evaluate and to make judgments. Students criticize and interpret, verify and judge, select and defend, look for inconsistency in writing, rank alternative solutions to a problem, and assess the weight of arguments in a piece of persuasive writing. For example, in teaching a history unit on how railroads contributed to the growth and development of North America, students may begin with an analysis and synthesis of why the railroads mushroomed and what they did for the country. To extend the experience, gifted students could evaluate the actions of the railroad robber barons who lobbied for political favors and exploited the free enterprise system. They could apply evaluative thinking in addressing such questions as: What might have been a better way for developing a transcontinental transportation system? Was there a legitimate justification for the government granting special favors to the railroads? Would they be justified for our transportation system today? Are there lessons from that era that apply to our modern interstate highway system or our space program?

The skills involved in analysis, synthesis, and evaluation are precisely the ones needed to challenge gifted students' intellectual and creative potential. While all students should have the opportunity to develop higher level thinking, for gifted students analysis, synthesis, and evaluation should be central elements in their learning activities.

Critical thinking tends to be convergent, with the objective of finding one right answer for a given problem or one best way to approach the problem. By contrast, creativity is a process of divergent thinking leading to a variety of approaches. Creative thinking has four primary characteristics: 1) originality, or innovative approaches to problems often involving the application of new ideas to old concepts; 2) fluency, or the capacity to generate many ideas for using a particular item or for solving a problem; 3) flexibility, or being open to or adaptable to changing conditions or circumstances; 4) elaboration, or expanding on initial ideas resulting in a product or solution to a problem that is quite different from what was originally intended (Renzulli 1986, p. 468). Gifted students should be given many opportunities to use both critical and creative thinking.

Individualized Instruction Options

In *Developing Talent in Young People* (1985), Benjamin Bloom reports that talented students usually have had a highly individualized relationship with a teacher or mentor. The teacher or mentor guides these students, provides encouragement, and facilitates independent study. Independent study, under the guidance of a teacher, allows gifted students to develop an individualized unit of study appropriate for their interests and abilities.

Starr Cline (1986) lists 12 steps in conducting independent study projects, starting with identification of a topic through completion of a product or performance. The steps are:

1. Student selects topic.
2. Teacher guides student in design of study.
3. Student learns appropriate skills for carrying out the design.
4. Teacher monitors outline of study prepared by student.
5. Student and teacher locate appropriate resources.
6. Student conducts research on topic.
7. Student narrows or expands topic if necessary.
8. Teacher allows sufficient time for research.
9. Student seeks teacher assistance if needed.
10. Student selects presentation method, for example, slide/sound show, videotape program, dramatization, chalk talk.
11. Student and teacher seek appropriate audiences for completed project (peers, parents, professionals, publications).
12. Student evaluates his or her performance.

Students who successfully complete independent study projects become, to some extent, experts on a specific topic. Giving them opportunities to share their "expertise" through some form of presentation enhances their self-concept and encourages them to pursue other topics.

Some teachers of the gifted express concern about students undertaking independent study projects, because without constant feedback students can get bogged down and make little progress. Others complain that continuous monitoring required with independent study projects is too demanding of teachers' time. However, once procedures have been established for conducting independent study projects and students become familiar with them, this form of individualized learning can be an important component of a gifted education program.

Mentoring is another form of individualized learning. Mentors are adult volunteers who teach, counsel, and inspire students with interests similar to their own. One successful mentoring program serving adolescents in the Columbus, Ohio, area is Learning Juncture, a nonprofit organization that regularly links mentors with students (Brenham 1987). This program allows students to spend six to eight hours each week with mentors whose profession, trade, or business matches the student's talent, interest, or career ambition. Each student keeps a journal and attends seminars dealing with personal goals and career expectations. The program lasts four months, the length of a semester. The student receives mentor evaluation, self-evaluation, and evaluation by seminar leader. The evaluation becomes a part of the student's permanent record and, if requested, is included with the student's college applications. Lester Jipp, executive director of Learning Juncture, maintains that the mentor relationship has lasting benefits for the student. Mentors frequently write letters of recommendation for college applications and for future job applications.

Creative Problem Solving

Creative Problem Solving (Isaksen and Treffinger 1985) is a seven-step process for identifying and solving problems. The seven steps are: 1) recognizing problems, 2) identifying data needed to solve problems, 3) posing alternative interpretations of the problems, 4) identifying related subproblems, 5) generating many new and unusual ideas for solving problems, 6) establishing criteria for analyzing and evaluating promising alternatives, and 7) formulating and successfully carrying out a specific plan of action.

Creative Problem Solving is a process that can be used with gifted students from kindergarten through high school. It can intrigue kindergartners with a problem such as a pet dragon who refuses to go to school. For high school

14

students the problem might be very realistic, such as being invited to a party where you know drugs will be used. *CPS for Kids* published by D.O.K. provides many activities for various age levels that can be used to initiate the program.

Multiple Talents Approach

Based on his research on creativity, Calvin Taylor (1968 *a* and *b*) has developed an instructional model that emphasizes both academic and creative talents. Taylor sees creative thinking as falling into eight categories: productive thinking, planning, communicating, forecasting, decision-making, implementing, human relations, and discerning opportunities. Historically, schools have acknowledged only academic success; but success in the real world requires multiple creative talents.

With appropriate teaching strategies and curriculum, teachers can develop the creative thinking talents of children. At the same time, by expanding the kinds of talents valued, many more children can be considered gifted in at least one or more of the creative thinking areas. In order to develop the creative thinking potential of each child, Taylor introduces the concept of a double curriculum wherein academic content and creative thinking talents are taught simultaneously. A teacher can begin by introducing one new talent into the academic curriculum. It does not matter which talent the teacher begins with. It could be one the teacher is most comfortable with, such as communicating or planning. The initial step may be to set aside five to ten minutes each day to teach one creative thinking strategy. Gradually, others can be added until all of them are integrated into all content areas.

With Taylor's approach, students change roles from passive receivers of information to active users of knowledge. They become "doers" rather than just "listeners." Learning is open-ended, with an emphasis on discovery, freedom of choice, and variety. Learning activities include planning, forecasting, and decision making. Students learn that there are many "right" ways of accomplishing a task or solving a problem.

Taylor's theory of multiple talents challenges traditional notions of gifted education in which students are selected solely on the basis of I.Q. and achievement test scores. Using his approach, as many as 30% to 50% of the student body might be considered gifted in one or more of the creative talent areas. Many educators welcome Taylor's approach and feel that it should be used in every classroom, not just for the gifted.

The Cognitive-Affective Model

The cognitive-affective model (Williams 1970) was not specifically designed for gifted children, but its emphasis on divergent thinking skills meshes nicely with the instructional strategies for the gifted. Williams sees learning as a process of making connections between a new experience and things already experienced. Williams refers to this as "connectedness." By using appropriate teaching strategies, students are able to make more and more connections.

The Williams' cognitive-affective model is illustrated by a cube. On one side is subject matter, another side is teacher behavior (teaching strategies), and the third side is pupil behavior. Subject matter is divided into the usual curriculum areas of art, music, science, social studies, mathematics, and language. The teacher behavior side presents 18 different teaching strategies to use with any of the curriculum areas. Some of those are: paradoxes, analogies, provocative questions, examples of change, skills of research, tolerance for ambiguity, study of creative people and processes, and intuitive expression. Application of the 18 different strategies to the six curriculum areas provides enormously varied learning experiences for gifted students.

Using these different teaching strategies, students are exposed to divergent thinking processes, which studies have shown are attributes of highly creative persons. Some of these attributes are:

1. Risk-taking: willingness to accept failure or criticism, capacity to speculate or take a guess, able to function under unstructured conditions, able to defend one's own ideas.

2. Complexity: tendency to delve into intricate problems or ideas, ability to see many alternatives, ability to see gaps between how things are and how they could be, ability to bring order out of unstructured situations.

3. Curiosity: capacity to wonder, be inquisitive, toy with ideas, open to puzzling situations, ponder the mystery of things, follow a particular hunch just to see what will happen.

4. Imagination: power to visualize and build mental images, dream about things that have never happened, make intuitive leaps, reach beyond existing boundaries.

Williams has compiled a package of books, tapes, inservice training materials, and other supplements, which school systems can use for their gifted education programs. Called the *Total Creativity Program Kit*, it is available from Educational Technology Publications, 140 Sylvan Avenue, Englewood Cliffs, NJ 07632.

The Integrative Model

Barbara Clark (1986), using findings from recent brain research, concludes that learning can be enhanced by using teaching strategies that integrate four brain functions. The first she identifies as the thinking or cognitive function, which is the analytic, sequential, and evaluative; also the capacity to generalize, conceptualize, and reason abstractly. The second brain function is the emotional or affective function, which Clark describes as the "gateway" to more advanced cognitive functions. The third is the physical or sensing function, which includes movement, physical encoding, sight, hearing, smell, taste, and touch. The fourth function is intuition or insight fulness. This last function is regarded with some suspicion in our Western culture because of its seeming lack of rationality. Nevertheless, it is the function that underlies creativity. According to Clark, intuition "is in use when it is felt that something is known, but it cannot be told how it was known. It is a sense of total understanding, of directly and immediately gaining a concept in its whole, living existence, and is in part the result of a high level of synthesis of all the brain functions" (p. 29).

Clark's integrative learning model seems particularly appropriate for the gifted classroom, but it will require different instructional approaches. Instead of making logical, rational thought the sole focus of instruction, there should be integration of all four brain functions including logical, emotional, sensing, and intuitive knowledge. Rather than using external tension such as tests and grades for motivation and control, she recommends the use of relaxation techniques including yoga and meditation to synchronize brain functions. Most class time should be spent on individualized instruction and small-group work, and the curriculum should be responsive to individual interests. Instead of focusing on recall of facts, the teacher should "present new ways of viewing facts, and eliciting new questions for as yet unresolved issues" (p. 32). Finally, teachers should use integrative techniques to empower students to be responsible for their own learning.

In *Optimizing Learning: The Integrative Education Model in the Classroom*, Clark describes the classroom climate, organization, and structure appropriate to integrative learning and gives examples of how the model can be used in a variety of educational settings from preschool through secondary school. She also provides sample lessons for different age levels to illustrate how each of the brain functions can be integrated into one lesson. Clark's integrative model provides many techniques the teacher of the gifted will want to try.

The Enrichment Triad/Revolving Door Model

The Enrichment Triad/Revolving Door Model (Renzulli 1986) provides a truly differentiated experience for gifted children. The model includes three types of activities. Students revolve from Type I activities to Type

II to Type III, and then begin over again. Type III activities are particularly appropriate for the gifted.

Type I activities in the Enrichment Triad include general exploratory experiences. Students are exposed to a variety of experiences in several fields of study not commonly found in the regular curriculum. Type I activities might be visiting speakers, field trips, demonstrations, or taped commercial television programs. The goal is to provide stimulating experiences that appeal to the interests of gifted students and that are appropriate for different learning styles. Visits with artists, engineers, newspaper reporters, and stock brokers should be more than a brief chat and a tour of the work site. Students should be encouraged to try their hand at some of the jobs these professionals do.

Type II activities in the Enrichment Triad are designed to develop the cognitive and affective functions. Specifically, they are intended to: 1) develop problem solving, critical thinking, and affective processes such as sensing, appreciating, and valuing; 2) develop specific learning-how-to-learn skills such as notetaking, interviewing, classifying and analyzing data, and drawing conclusions; 3) develop skills in the use of reference sources such as readers' guides, directories, abstracts, etc.; 4) develop written, oral, and visual communication skills in order to create products for a designated audience. Type II activities are an integral part of the school curriculum and should not be considered a "frill."

Renzulli defines Type III enrichment as "investigative activities and artistic productions in which the learner assumes the role of a firsthand inquirer; the student thinking, feeling, and acting like a practicing professional" (p. 250). The objectives of Type III activities are:

1. To provide students opportunities to apply their interests, knowledge, creative ideas, and task commitment to a self-selected problem or area of study;
2. To acquire in-depth understanding of the content and methodology associated with a particular discipline, area of artistic expression, and interdisciplinary studies;
3. To develop original products for use with a specified audience;
4. To develop skills in the areas of planning, organization, resource utilization, time management, decision-making, and self-evaluation;
5. To develop task commitment, self-confidence, sense of accomplishment, and the ability to interact effectively with others who share the student's interest and expertise.

Before students undertake a Type III activity, the teacher must assess whether they have the commitment to follow through with it. A Type III project should represent original work, not the traditional report based on information from an encyclopedia. Students should be gathering their own data. This means attending meetings, interviewing experts, conducting surveys, building models, doing experiments, and reading original works. The teacher must wear many hats in the process, including that of research assistant, motivator, and champion of the cause.

Conclusion

Many of the teaching strategies for the gifted described here have similar objectives; the interrelatedness of creative and cognitive learning is a common theme. Although experts suggest different strategies for similar objectives, they are not mutually exclusive. For example, there is no reason why Type III enrichment projects could not occur in a gifted class using Barbara Clark's integrative model. New approaches will continue to evolve as teachers work with the variety of learning styles and thinking processes exhibited by gifted children.

References

Bloom, B., ed. *Developing Talent in Young People*. New York: Ballantine, 1985.

Bloom, B. *The Taxonomy of Educational Objectives: The Classification of Educational Goals. Handbook I: Cognitive Domain*. New York: David McKay, 1956.

Brenham, T. "Worthington Program Helps Teens Learn About Jobs, Gain School Credit," *Columbus Dispatch*, 24 July 1987

Clark, B. *Optimizing Learning: The Integrative Education Model in the Classroom*. Columbus, Ohio: Charles E. Merrill, 1986.

Cline, S. *The Independent Learner: A Guide to Creative Independent Study*. East Aurora, N.Y.: D.O.K., 1986.

Costa, A., ed. *Developing Minds: A Resource Book for Teaching Thinking*. Alexandria, Va.: Association for Supervision and Curriculum Development, 1985.

Isaksen, S., and Treffinger, D. *Creative Problem Solving: The Basic Course*. Buffalo, N.Y.: Bearly, 1985.

Maker, C. *Teaching Models in Education of the Gifted*. Rockville, Md.: Aspen Teaching Systems, 1982.

Meeker, M. "SOI." In *Developing Minds: A Resource Book for Teaching Thinking*, edited by A. Costa. Alexandria, Va.: Association for Supervision and Curriculum Development, 1985.

Nash, D., and Treffinger, D. *The Mentor*. East Aurora, N.Y.: D.O.K., 1986.

Renzulli, J.S., ed. *Systems and Models for Developing Programs for the Gifted and Talented*. Mansfield Center, Conn.: Creative Learning Press, 1986.

Stein, M.I. *Gifted, Talented, and Creative Young People*. New York: Garland, 1986.

Taylor, C.W. "The Multiple Talent Approach." *Instructor* 77 (1968): 142-46. a

Taylor, C.W. "Be Talent Developers as Well as Knowledge Dispensers." *Today's Education* 57 (1968): 67-69. b

Treffinger, D.; Feldhusen, J.; and Hohn, R. *Reach Each You Teach*. East Aurora, N.Y.: D.O.K., 1986.

Williams, F.E. *Classroom Ideas for Encouraging Thinking and Feeling*, 2nd ed. East Aurora, N.Y.: D.O.K., 1970.

CHAPTER THREE
Organizing the Gifted Program

There are many factors to consider when initiating a gifted program. Usually a school district appoints a committee or task force to develop a written plan that serves as an operational guide for implementing the program. The written plan should address the following areas:

- Program philosophy
- Program goals and objectives
- Population to be served
- Admission criteria
- Program budget
- Program structure and design
- Staffing and staff responsibilities
- Facilities, schedules, materials, and supplies
- Implementation procedures
- Program evaluation

The committee or task force appointed to develop the written plan generally includes district and building administrators, the gifted education coordinator, parent and teacher representatives, selected support service personnel (for example, a librarian, learning center director, school social worker, or psychologist), and, if already selected, those teachers who will be directly involved in the gifted program. If the gifted program includes the secondary schools, it may be appropriate to invite a student representative to serve on the committee. The committee should represent persons with diverse experiences and points of view but who share a commitment to education of the gifted.

The committee may wish to consider hiring a consultant to assist in developing program objectives and program design. An outside expert can be an invaluable asset during the planning stage. State departments, local universities, and professional organizations in gifted education are sources for securing recommendations of qualified consultants.

During the planning stage, it is important that the committee establish a timeline for completing its work. A timeline serves as a form of discipline for the committee and helps to maintain momentum during the planning period. Some committees distribute the workload by assigning different members to do the research and make recommendations in particular areas. In other instances, the principal or district staff person, the gifted coordinator, and the consultant assume primary responsibility for research and design. Under this organization, the committee serves as a deliberative body that reviews, critiques, and gives final approval for the plan.

A good starting point for the committee is to review existing state guidelines and regulations governing gifted education programs. The committee also might want to visit gifted programs in nearby school districts. Conducting a questionnaire survey is an efficient way of soliciting input from the teaching staff, administrators, parents, and students concerning the proposed program.

Selecting a Target Population

Early in the planning, the committee must identify the target population to be served by the gifted program. Often the target population will emerge while the committee is formulating its philosophy and objectives. For example, if the program is to have a math/science orientation, then the target population will be limited to students with high achievement in these content areas. Another program might focus on the arts, and the target population would be those students gifted in the visual or performing arts. What is important is that program objectives and the target population be compatible.

Establishing Admission Criteria

Having selected the target population the program will serve, the committee must then develop specific criteria for admitting students into the gifted program. This is a challenging task. Although established federal and state guidelines are helpful, it is important to develop specific admission criteria based on the demonstrated needs of the population to be served. Most schools use some form of standardized testing instrument as an initial indicator of student ability. However, as discussed in Chapter One, test scores should not be the sole criterion for program nomination, much less admission. Teacher checklists, peer nomination, self-nomination, and parent observations also should be considered.

22

Preliminary screening, typically revealing about 15% of the student body, should be followed up with more in-depth evaluation. This second stage of assessment might include a review of standardized test data, a review of students' academic history, and consultation with teachers and such support personnel as psychologists, counselors, and administrators. It is at this stage that individually administered tests might be used. Giving a weight to data from several sources provides a statistical profile for each candidate, which helps to make the admission process both more objective and more efficient.

Specific admission criteria will vary from school to school or district to district, reflecting the nature of the program and the community. Remind teachers that nominations for the program must not be limited to "good test-takers" or "teacher-pleasers." Gifted students are not necessarily the most academically successful or well behaved.

It is important that the admission criteria be spelled out in writing and be available for review by anyone concerned. By having the criteria in writing, teachers and administrators can refer to them when dealing with the inevitable questions from parents of "Why my child?" or "Why not my child?" Candidates who come close to the cut-off point for admission to the gifted program can be placed on a waiting list and re-evaluated at a later date.

Some procedural issues the admission criteria should address are:

1. If a vacancy occurs, how can a qualified student be moved into the program?
2. If a qualified transfer student comes in mid-year, can the student be admitted into the program? Does a new student "bump" other students who may have been on a waiting list for several months?
3. If a student wishes to leave the program, is parental permission required? Can students who leave the program change their minds and be accepted back into the program? Will these students be given priority over others who are on the waiting list?

Funding the Gifted Program

The size and nature of the gifted program will depend heavily on the funding available. The committee will have to consider funding at every step in the planning process. The first step is determining if funds are available from the state and, if so, the procedures for obtaining them. The second step is determining the funding available from the district in the regular budget. Other sources of funding might be found in the community. Some programs receive financial assistance from business sponsors. Others may be partially subsidized by local colleges or universities.

23

Gifted Program Models

There are many models of gifted programming. They vary in structure and design. The most common models in elementary school are discussed in this chapter. Preprimary and secondary programs are discussed in Chapters Five and Nine.

Pull-Out Programs. In pull-out programs, children leave their heterogeneous classroom for a specified time each week to participate in a special class with their gifted peers. One survey found that 70% of districts with gifted programs had pull-out programs (Cox, Daniel, and Boston 1985).

The popularity of pull-out programs is probably because they are relatively easy to implement (Belcastro 1987). A chief advantage of pull-out programs is that gifted students have the opportunity to interact with other gifted students as well as with their regular classmates. Another advantage is that during the period the gifted students are out of the regular classroom, the teacher has more time to work individually with the remaining students. In addition, those students who frequently are overshadowed by their gifted classmates are given an opportunity to shine. A final advantage is that, since the regular teacher covers instruction in basic skills, the teacher of the gifted in the pull-out sessions is free to focus on critical and creative thinking skills.

For regular classroom teachers, the pull-out model has some inherent frustrations. With basic content and skill instruction taking most of their time, teachers may feel disheartened when hearing about the more exciting activities of the pull-out class. The periodic departure of the gifted students from the classroom can be disruptive and cause scheduling problems.

The students who remain in the regular classroom may resent the absence of their classmates. Even if that is not the case, gifted students might react negatively to their involvement in the pull-out program. During time away from their regular classroom, gifted students may miss the introduction of new material. Also, the combination of regular homework, make up of missed assignments, plus the special pull-out class projects may become overwhelming to gifted students, which can dampen their original enthusiasm for the program.

Probably the fundamental defect of the pull-out model is that it offers a "part-time solution to a full-time problem" (Cox, Daniel, and Boston 1985, p. 43). A pull-out program may meet gifted students' needs during the hours of special instruction, but most of their time is still spent in a less challenging learning environment.

Clustering Model. Clustering is a program model in which gifted students function as a small group within a single heterogeneous classroom.

24

Like pull-out programs, clustering is easy to implement. The classroom teacher is responsible for planning and implementing the program for the gifted cluster, although in some instances the gifted program coordinator may help with curriculum design and project activities. The success of this model is highly dependent on the classroom management skills of the teacher. This model works best where instruction is essentially individualized.

In the cluster model, gifted students profit from extended contact with their intellectual peers but are not singled out as much as they are in pull-out programs. It is common for gifted students to move in and out of the cluster group, depending on the nature of the learning activity and the changing needs of the students. The major disadvantage of the model is that the demands of basic classroom instruction are such that cluster programming is often limited to brief periods that the teacher can spare from the day's schedule.

Combination Cluster/Pull-Out. Some of the disadvantages of both pull-out and clustering can be overcome by using a combination of these models. Schools or districts opting for the pull-out model should seriously consider using it in tandem with clustering. Students participating in the combined program have more time with their gifted peers; there is less disruption of the regular classroom; and the gifted teacher or coordinator is able to devote more time to building strong, collaborative relationships with the regular teachers (Eby and Smutny 1990, p. 146).

Special Classes. According to a survey, less than 40% of districts with gifted programs offer full-time special classes for gifted students (Cox, Daniel, and Boston 1985). This model offers several advantages. Most significantly, special classes address the needs of gifted students on a full-time basis. Thinking skills can be taught in the context of the various content areas; long-term project activities are more feasible; individualization and acceleration are easier to implement; and teachers and students have time to develop closer working relationships. However, having a special full-time classroom for the gifted provides no guarantee of a good gifted program unless the learning environment is structured appropriately, the curriculum is well designed, and the teachers are adequately prepared.

Special Schools. There are many kinds of special schools for the gifted. Some are sponsored by districts, some by regions, and some even by states. Others are independent or affiliated with colleges and universities. Some special schools operate as schools-within-schools with their own programming and staff but physically housed in the same building as the regular students. At the secondary level, special schools may focus on specific content areas, for example, the performing arts, math and science, or foreign languages.

Special schools can offer a wealth of program possibilities because the scheduling, curriculum, and even the physical structure of the school can be focused on the needs of gifted students. Also, special schools offer the advantage of having all the resources (teachers, equipment, and materials) in one place. A further advantage of the special school is that it can serve an ethnically diverse student body.

References

Belcastro, F. "Elementary Pull-Out Program for the Intellectually Gifted: Boon or Bane?" *Roeper Review* 9, no. 4 (1987): 208-12.

Cox, J., and Daniel, N. "The Pull-Out Model." *G/C/T* 34 (1984): 55-61.

Cox, J.; Daniel, N.; and Boston, B. *Educating Able Learners*. Austin: University of Texas Press, 1985.

Davis, G.A., and Rimm, S.B. *Education of the Gifted and Talented*. Englewood Cliffs, N.J.: Prentice-Hall, 1989.

Eby, J.W., and Smutny, J.F. *A Thoughtful Overview of Gifted Education*. White Plains, N.Y.: Longman, 1990.

Johnson, N. "Cluster Grouping in the Regular Classroom." Paper presented at the Sixth Annual Conference of the American Association of Gifted Children on "Supporting Emotional Needs of Gifted Children," Arlington Heights, Ill., 1987.

Orenstein, A. "Organizational Characteristics Are Important in Planning, Implementing and Maintaining Programs for the Gifted." *Gifted Child Quarterly* 28, no. 3 (1984): 99-103.

CHAPTER FOUR
Building Support
for the Gifted Program

The success of any gifted program depends on many factors, including program design and implementation, student selection, teacher effectiveness, and administrative support. But critical to the establishment of a gifted program is developing constituencies among parents, teachers, and the community-at-large. This chapter suggests strategies for building bridges to each of these constituencies and engaging their active support.

Building Parent Support

When initiating a gifted program, information about it and the student selection process should be distributed to every parent, not just to those parents whose children are likely candidates for the program. Limiting the information about the program to a selective group is sure to brand the program as "exclusive" and "elitist." When the organizing committee has completed its written plan, the school should schedule an open forum to which all parents are invited. The written plan should be available for inspection, and plenty of time should be reserved for parents' questions.

When communicating with parents, it is important to explain that there are many types of giftedness and that any single program can address only a few of these types. Parents also need to understand the distinction between giftedness and academic success. Although there is a positive correlation between the two, they are not necessarily the same. Also, it should be pointed out that, although only a small percentage of students will participate directly in the gifted program, elements of the program (for example, teacher training and curricular innovations) can benefit the entire school population. The person presenting information about the program to parents should be prepared to illustrate several ways in which the gifted program will benefit the general student body.

After the gifted program is under way, information about it can be presented in the context of the district's total educational offerings and services. For example, an orientation meeting for parents of kindergartners or for students transferring into the district is a good time to discuss all the school's special educational opportunities, of which the gifted program is one.

The gifted program staff should maintain regular contact with the parents of children participating in the program. Through regular contact, parents develop a better understanding of their child's special educational needs and, in the process, they become strong advocates of gifted programs not only for their own child but for all children with special talents. Also, parents of gifted children can be involved as volunteers for various projects connected with the program.

Involving Parents as Volunteers

There are many ways to involve parents as volunteers in a gifted program. The volunteer program should be flexible, allowing parents with diverse skills and interests to contribute as their time and schedules allow. Some volunteer activities will require that parents be available during the school day; many others can occur outside of classroom time. Following are some ways in which parents can be involved as volunteers:

1. Organizing or participating in local parent support groups for the gifted.
2. Attending national, regional, or state conferences on gifted education and sharing ideas about programming learned from such conferences.
3. Becoming a spokesperson for the gifted program by making presentations at school board meetings, service clubs, and parent groups.
4. Assisting the teacher in the classroom in activities requiring a low student-adult ratio.
5. Becoming involved in a mentor program with one or more students who share a common interest.
6. Developing instructional materials. This may range from laminating and duplicating to designing instructional games or developing independent study units in an area in which a parent has expertise.
7. Organizing a library of materials about gifted children and gifted education. Often this can be done cooperatively with a school or public library.
8. Accompanying a class or smaller groups of students on field trips or assisting in planning off-campus experiences.
9. Participating in fund-raising for the program. In the course of raising money for special equipment or field trips, parents raise the program's visibility in the community.
10. Editing or writing for a newsletter or journal on gifted students.

In addition to parents, grandparents and other senior citizens with special talents to contribute to the program can be recruited as volunteers. The interaction of gifted students with older adults can be a mutually rewarding experience and provides another avenue for developing community understanding about the importance of special programs for gifted children.

Building Community Support

Community support is necessary to get a gifted program off the ground and, once established, to protect it when threatened by budget cuts. Support can come from a variety of sources and in a variety of ways, but it must be solicited. More often than not, community support is the result of carefully nurtured relationships requiring a considerable amount of time and energy.

Sources of community support include interested individuals, businesses, civic groups, and social service agencies. The nature of the support will vary. Mentorships, in-kind donations, equipment loans, the use of facilities, and contributions of staff time are some possible options.

Des Moines, Iowa, is one school system that recognizes the importance of enlisting parents to help build community support for its gifted program (DeVries 1987, Roets 1989). This system has hired a professional to coordinate the effort. This person serves as a community resource consultant to bring gifted students resources beyond the classroom. Community members are recruited to work with students in a variety of ways. In some instances, an adult is asked to meet one time with one student. Other adults work on a weekly basis with a group of students. Other community members provide auxiliary services such as judging competitions, organizing and managing programs, or making phone calls.

In the Des Moines program, activities occur during the school day, late afternoon, Saturdays, or in the summer. Mentors in math, writing, or music composition come into the school. Students can apprentice in a television studio, stockbroker's office, veterinary clinic, law firm, or an architect's office. Professional organizations host all-day workshops. Special classes are held on college campuses. Cooperative programs are arranged with local art centers, community playhouses, science centers, or the botanical gardens.

One of the best ways of winning community support for gifted programs is through exhibits and performances. These events provide a forum for gifted students to share their best efforts with relatives and friends and offer tangible evidence of the value of the gifted program. Public visibility of the creative talents of gifted youngsters sends a positive message about the quality of the schools and will be of interest to the local economic development office, board of realtors, and other groups that want to attract people and businesses to locate in the community.

Developing Teacher Awareness and Support

In building support for the gifted program among teachers, it is important initially to work with all the teachers in the system, not just those who will be directly involved. The gifted program staff will likely be those with special training and experience in the field, but regular classroom teachers also should have a thorough grounding in the theory and practice of gifted education. Nancy Johnson (1987) makes a distinction between a *gifted program* and *gifted education*. A gifted program is the responsibility of a few designated people (administrator, coordinator, and teacher), while gifted education is everyone's job. It is Johnson's firm belief that comprehensive, articulated gifted education requires the involvement of teachers at all levels.

A series of workshops or inservice sessions led by an outside consultant can provide a general overview of gifted education for all teachers. An informal survey of teachers can determine what topics in gifted education are of most interest to them.

Teachers of the gifted themselves can be good agents for developing support for the program from their peers. Barbara Clark (1988) provides these suggestions for building support among the teaching staff as well as finding support in other sources:

1. Watch for those teachers who are interested in what you are doing, invite them into your room, share your materials and ideas, and ask them for their opinions.
2. Take every opportunity to let the entire faculty know they are welcome at any time to visit, participate, share ideas, or have their students work with your students.
3. Discuss what you are doing with the principal and other administrators and invite their participation.
4. Keep parents informed about your goals and activities and invite their participation.
5. Do not overlook the custodians and office staff. Both can provide invaluable support; they understand how the school operates and know how to get things done that can never be learned from those "in charge."
6. Attend workshops, conferences, and university classes on gifted education. There you will meet others who share your interests.

Seeking Support from Administrative Personnel

Administrative support from principals, the superintendent, and school board members is extremely important to the success of the gifted program and needs to be cultivated. These persons need to be well informed about the program because they may be called on to field questions, particularly about the student identification and selection process and program content. Early and continuing contact with administrators by the gifted teacher or coordinator helps when problems arise.

The interest and involvement of administrators vary. Some may wish to participate in every phase of the program, including student selection and curriculum development; others take a less active role but want to be kept informed through monthly or quarterly reports.

Conclusion

Gifted education advocates often work hard to build initial support for a new program but underestimate the need for continuing support from parents, teachers, administrators, and the community. Sustained support is vital to the preservation of the gifted program, because it is often perceived as a "frill" and is among the first programs threatened when a district faces budget cuts. The more parents, teachers, administrators, and community members are able to testify to the efficacy of the gifted program, the better its chances for survival.

References

Clark, B. *Growing Up Gifted*. 3rd ed. Columbus, Ohio: Charles E. Merrill, 1988.

DeVries, A. "Community Caring for the Gifted." Paper presented at the Sixth Annual Conference of the American Association of Gifted Children on "Supporting the Emotional Needs of Gifted Children," Arlington Heights, Ill., 1987.

Johnson, N. "Cluster Grouping in the Regular Classroom." Paper presented at the Sixth Annual Conference of the American Association of Gifted Children on "Supporting the Emotional Needs of Gifted Children," Arlington Heights, Ill., 1987.

Orenstein, A. "What Organizational Characteristics Are Important in Planning, Implementing, and Maintaining Programs for the Gifted." *Gifted Child Quarterly* 28, no. 3 (1984): 99-103.

Roets, L.F., ed. *Gifted and Talented Program Description*. Des Moines Public Schools, 1800 Grade Avenue, Des Moines, Iowa 50307, 1989.

CHAPTER FIVE
Preschool Gifted Children

There is ample evidence that gifted preschoolers can be identified; and, like their older cohorts, they have special needs. If these needs are unrecognized or ignored, these children are likely to find the preschool program unchallenging or even boring. Unfortunately, few school districts have any special programming to serve these children. Moreover, early childhood teachers are not trained to identify and challenge these children in the regular classroom; and teachers of the gifted typically are not accustomed to working with very young children.

With a few exceptions, public school education in this country begins at age five. The vast majority of preschool programs are independently sponsored. With the exception of Head Start, there has been very little federal funding for preschool programs. Special programming for the gifted is beyond the means of most independent preschools, which understandably have focused their programs on the needs of the average child. Despite these limiting factors, there is much that can be done in preschool programs for the gifted.

Programming for the preschool gifted should not be confused with what some have called the "super baby" approach. This approach typically emphasizes formal instruction using flash cards, workbooks, and repetitive drills to teach reading and writing as well as fact-filled content such as identifying and memorizing the instruments in a symphony orchestra. This type of rote learning is unrelated to the preschooler's experience and has no place in the gifted education program for young children.

Gifted education for preschoolers should be firmly grounded in the developmental tradition of early childhood education. It should include experiences designed to encourage children to explore actively the world around them. It should be structured so that children are free to move about the classroom and select their own activities. Of course, the same basic principles apply to the preschool child at home where experiential learning is emphasized.

Identifying Gifted Preschoolers

There is no reason to identify gifted preschoolers simply for identification's sake. The identification process should be designed with a particular program in mind. For example, the identification process for a preschool program focusing on music and art should focus on young children who appear to be gifted in those areas. In preschools with no special gifted program emphasis but with a desire to provide more challenging programs for gifted children, a teacher might complete a behavioral checklist (described later) for each child and request parents to use the same checklist to record their observations of their child.

For formal programming, Karnes (1983) suggests a "multiple-entry-point" identification process, which offers children a variety of avenues for entering a special program. This differs from sequential approaches using a nomination process, group testing, or other screening instrument, followed by individual testing.

The RAPYHT project at the University of Illinois serves handicapped gifted preschoolers (Karnes, Shwedel, and Lewis 1983). Each child's teacher and parent fills out a series of talent checklists. The checklists cover a variety of abilities including creative, intellectual, scientific, mathematical, reading, musical, leadership, artistic, and psychomotor. If children are rated above a predetermined cut-off point in any of the areas, they are eligible to participate in small-group activities in their area(s) of strength. If the children perform adequately in one or two activities, they are allowed to enroll in a supplemental program.

Gowan (1975) provides another example of the multiple-entry point approach. In this approach, candidates are identified using aptitude tests, teacher nominations, and selection committee nominations. This information provides children with three ways to enter the gifted program: 1) by scoring high on aptitude tests, 2) by receiving recommendations and scoring above the cut-off score on an I.Q. test, or 3) through special consideration by the selection committee. This multiple-entry identification approach uses different sources of information to assess a range of abilities. Such an approach can be adapted for use with preschoolers.

Individually administered tests frequently used with young children include the Draw-A-Person Test (Harris), the Stanford-Binet (Terman & Merrill), Thinking Creatively in Action and Movement (Torrance), and the Wechsler Preschool Primary Scale of Intelligence. In addition, there are several tests or instruments that assess intelligence, achievement, and social/emotional and perceptual/motor development. Karnes (1983) suggests the following tests for use with preschool children:

Intelligence Tests
   The Columbia Mental Maturity Scale
   The Slosson Intelligence Test for Children and Adults
   The Pictorial Test of Intelligence

Achievement Tests
   The Metropolitan Readiness Test, Level 1
   Stanford Early Achievement Test, Level 1
   Test of Basic Experiences, Level K

Tests of Perceptual-Motor Development
   Basic Motor Ability Test
   Developmental Test of Visual-Motor Integration
   Purdue Perceptual-Motor Survey

Tests of Social Development
   California Preschool Competency Scale
   Vineland Social Maturity Scale

Tests of Creativity
   Torrance Tests of Creative Thinking: Figural Test
   Torrance Tests of Creative Thinking: Verbal Test
   Thinking Creatively in Action and Movement

For information about each of these instruments, consult *Buros Mental Measurement Yearbook*, which is available at most university or large public libraries. Keep in mind, however, that even the most exhaustive battery of tests will not provide a complete picture of a child's abilities and may actually give an inaccurate view in some cases.

Checklists of behavioral characteristics and parent and teacher questionnaires have proven to be practical and inclusive methods of identification and deserve a place in every identification process. A number of behavioral characteristic lists exist. The list below is Margie Kitano's (1982) synthesis of the work of several researchers. It is important to note that no gifted preschooler is likely to exhibit all of these behaviors. It is more common to find behaviors clustered in one or two of the five areas listed below.

Intellectual/Academic Behaviors
   • is attentive, alert
   • possesses advanced vocabulary for age
   • shows early interest in books and reading
   • learns rapidly
   • has high level of curiosity
   • enjoys being with older children

34

- pursues interests; collects things
- has a long attention span
- possesses high standards
- shows mature sense of humor for age
- prefers new and challenging experiences
- retains information
- displays high level of planning, problem solving, and abstract thinking compared to peers

Creative Behaviors
- asks many questions
- does things in own way, is independent
- may prefer to work alone
- experiments with whatever is at hand
- is highly imaginative
- thinks up many ways to accomplish a goal
- may respond with unexpected answers, sometimes smart alecky
- produces original ideas

Leadership Behaviors
- is frequently sought out by peers
- interacts easily with other children and adults
- adapts easily to new situations
- can influence others to work toward goals – desirable or undesirable
- is looked to by others for ideas and decisions
- is chosen first by peers

Musical Behaviors
- makes up original tunes
- shows degree of tonal memory
- enjoys musical activities
- responds sensitively to music
- easily repeats rhythm patterns
- easily discriminates tones, melodies, rhythm patterns

Artistic Behaviors
- fills extra time by drawing, painting, etc.
- draws a variety of things – not just people, houses, and flowers
- remembers things in detail
- takes art activities seriously and derives satisfaction from them
- has long attention span when engaged in art activities
- shows planning in composing artwork

In addition to asking parents to complete a behavioral checklist, it is desirable to include parent interviews as part of any identification process. In fact, the interview gives parents an opportunity to discuss their checklist responses and describe specific anecdotes about their child's behavior, which the teacher may not be aware of in the classroom. It is important to note that research indicates that parents are more accurate in assessing their children's ability than teachers (Roedell, Jackson, and Robinson 1980). Parents are often aware of gifted behaviors that do not show up in the classroom.

Options in Preschool Programming for the Gifted

When designing programs for gifted preschoolers, the primary goal, of course, is to provide them with challenging educational experiences. But it is also important to include activities in the program that are designed to support parents. It is the rare parent who is adequately prepared to raise a gifted child. The school can help parents supplement and reinforce what the school is doing by suggesting appropriate activities and resources that can be used at home.

Cluster Grouping

In this program option, gifted preschoolers are clustered in a heterogeneous classroom. This option is easier to implement and is more practical when there are not enough gifted children to justify a separate special class. The cost of implementing this option is relatively low. In addition to staff salaries, funds will be needed for identification, parent education, inservice training, and equipment and supplies. An important benefit of this model is that it provides gifted children with opportunities for extended interaction with their intellectual peers and with the rest of the children in the class. This option allows gifted children to move in and out of a special cluster (often self-selected) based on a given activity's appropriateness for their abilities and needs.

This program model is not without its disadvantages. Teachers must have training in both early childhood and gifted education. And they must be able to develop learning activities that are appropriate for both gifted and regular students. If the gifted program is implemented in only a few of the schools in the district, parents must be willing to send their children to some place other than their neighborhood school.

Special Classes

This program option is not feasible unless there is a sufficient number of gifted students to justify a separate class. Therefore, it is unlikely that this option could be implemented in an independent preschool with only one class for each age level. However, it is feasible for districts with a large preschool or kindergarten enrollment. Special homogeneous classes provide gifted students with continuous contact with their highly intelligent and creative peers. With an entire class of gifted children, it is easier to integrate parent education into the program. Some schools even require that parents attend a workshop as a prerequisite to their child's enrollment in the special class.

One problem in implementing the special class option is finding early childhood teachers with training and experience in working with gifted young children. Another problem is that unless extended day care and school-operated transportation is provided, many children may not be able to participate in half-day special preschool classes.

A variation of the special class is a special school for the preschool gifted. These are usually private schools or are affiliated with a university but are not common. They have the added benefit of more flexible grouping and the concentration of materials and resources in a single facility. Examples of gifted preschools are the Creative Children's Academy in Illinois, the Eldorado School in California, and the Roeper School in Michigan.

Kindergarten Pull-Out Programs

The pull-out model at the kindergarten level operates very much like elementary pull-out programs (see Chapter Three). Gifted children are removed from their regular classroom on a regular schedule to attend special classes with their gifted peers. The disadvantages of elementary pull-out programs are amplified at the kindergarten level. If gifted children spend five hours a week of a typical half-day kindergarten in a pull-out program, this amounts to about a third of their time away from their regular class. Moreover, the pull-out gifted instructors tend to be the same persons who work with the school's older gifted students and are unlikely to have training in early childhood education. There is also a tendency for pull-out programs at this level to focus on formal instruction in reading, writing, and computation rather than on exploratory experiences, which are more appropriate for young children.

Partial Acceleration into First Grade

In some communities, socially mature and academically able kindergarten children spend some of their morning in a first-grade classroom. For young children who are able to function socially with older students, this may prove to be an alternative to being bored or unchallenged in kindergarten. However, by moving back and forth between classrooms, children may miss worthwhile activities going on in kindergarten while participating in a first-grade reading or math group. A better option is to modify the kindergarten curriculum to provide challenging opportunities for the gifted children.

Challenging the Preschool Gifted in the Regular Classroom

It is unrealistic to expect that there will be special classes available for the nation's gifted preschoolers; yet most preschool teachers have had gifted children in their classes at one time or another. Kitano (1982) contends that a skillful teacher can structure a regular preschool classroom to make it a nurturing place for every member of the class, including the gifted. She offers these recommendations:

1. Provide activities that cultivate creativity and foster fluency, flexibility, originality, and elaboration. For example, let children provide the ending of an unfinished story.

2. Provide activities that involve higher cognitive processes, such as analysis, synthesis, evaluation. Kitano gives an example using a discussion about colors. What colors does the artist use to create a strong feeling or emotion (analysis)? Paint a picture in which you use colors to create a strong feeling (synthesis). How well do you think you used certain colors to create a strong feeling (evaluation)?

3. Provide activities that involve planning, forecasting, and decision making. Situational problem solving incorporates these operations and is a satisfying exercise for gifted young children. An example is planning and building a model city of blocks that includes all the infrastructures and services (schools, fire department, post office, parks) found in a modern city.

4. Provide activities that promote inquiry. Encourage inductive thinking through the scientific process. Accept the hypotheses children offer and then let them test their hypotheses. For example, take a glass of water that is almost full and ask the children to guess how many pennies can be dropped into the glass before it overflows.

5. Provide activities that promote affective development. Young gifted children are concerned with issues of right and wrong, with what is fair and unfair. Give them opportunities to discuss incidents from their own experience that relate to these types of issues.

6. Provide opportunities for children to use a variety of thinking processes when dealing with the content of units or projects.

Staffing Preschool Gifted Programs

Staffing a preschool gifted program requires persons with training and experience in early childhood education and in gifted education. Also, a good sense of humor and a spirit of adventure are valuable assets. Because most teachers of gifted preschoolers will be working in regular classrooms, they must be able to individualize instruction in order to deal with a broad range of interests and abilities. Finally, they must be committed to working closely with parents, who need guidance in providing enriching experiences for their gifted children.

A Good Beginning for Young Gifted Children

Special programming, based on developmentally appropriate experiences, provides a good beginning for young gifted children and should be the first step in a comprehensive plan for the gifted. For most schools this special programming will have to be integrated into the regular early childhood classroom. This program model is not only easier to implement but is probably a sounder approach than pull-out or acceleration models. However, before any program model is implemented, there must be well-trained early childhood teachers who are skilled in identifying the gifted young and creative in providing challenging experiences that are appropriate for meeting their unique needs.

References

Abraham, W. *Living with Preschoolers*. Phoenix, Ariz.: O'Sullivan Woodside, 1976.

Bloom, B. *Taxonomy of Educational Objectives: The Classification of Educational Goals*. New York: David McKay, 1956.

Blocksom, R.H. *Nurturing Early Promise*. Bend, Ore.: Pinnaroo Publishing, 1989.

Blocksom, R. "Preschool Gifted Programs." *Illinois Council for the Gifted Journal* 4 (1985).

Clark, B. *Growing Up Gifted*, 3rd ed. Columbus, Ohio: Charles E. Merrill, 1988.

Clark, B. *Optimizing Learning: The Integrative Education Model in the Classroom*. Columbus, Ohio: Charles E. Merrill, 1986.

Gowan, J.C. *Trance, Art and Creativity*. Buffalo N.Y.: Creative Education Foundation, 1975.

Hall, E., and Skinner, N. *Somewhere to Turn: Strategies for Parents of the Gifted and Talented*. New York: Teachers College Press, 1980.

Karnes, M., ed. *The Underserved: Our Young Gifted Children*. Reston, Va.: Council for Exceptional Children, 1983.

Karnes, M.B., and Bertsch, J.D. "Identifying and Educating G/T Nonhandicapped and Handicapped Preschoolers." *Teaching Young Children* 10 (1978): 114-19.

Karnes, M.; Shwedel, A.; and Lewis, G. "Long-Term Effects of Early Programming for the Gifted/Talented Handicapped." *Journal for the Education of the Gifted* 6, no. 4 (1983): 266-78.

Karnes, M.; Schwedel, A.; and Williams, M. "Combining Instructional Models for Young Gifted Children." *Teaching Exceptional Children* 15, no. 3 (1983): 128-35.

Karnes, M.B., et al. *Preschool Talent Checklists Manual*. Urbana: Institute for Child Behavior and Development, University of Illinois, 1978.

Kitano, M. "Issues and Problems in Establishing Preschool Programs for the Gifted." *Roeper Review* 7, no. 4 (1985): 212-13.

Kitano, M. "Young Gifted Children: Strategies for Preschool Teachers." *Young Children* (May 1982): 14-24.

McHardy, R. "Planning for Preschool Gifted Education." *G/C/T* (September/October 1983): 24-27.

Roedell, W.; Jackson, N.; and Robinson, H. *Gifted Young Children*. New York: Teachers College Press, 1980.

Roeper, A. "The Young Gifted Child." *Gifted Child Quarterly* 21, no. 3 (1977): 388-96.

Seefeldt, C. "Tomorrow's Kindergarten: Pleasure or Pressure." *Principal* (May 1985): 12-15.

Smutny, J.F.; Veenker, S.; and Veenker, K. *Your Gifted Child*. New York: Facts on File, 1989.

CHAPTER SIX
Gifted Girls:
A Population at Risk

Almost 50 years ago J.R.R. Tolkein wrote: "How quickly an intelligent woman can be taught, grasp the teacher's ideas, see his point — and how (with some exceptions) they can go no further, when they leave his hand or when they lose interest in him. It is their gift to be receptive, stimulated, fertilized (in many other matters than the physical) by the male" (quoted in *The Inklings* by H. Carpenter).

Today Tolkein's words seem more amusing than insulting; and we are tempted to congratulate ourselves on the progress we have made during the second half of the twentieth century regarding the status of women. Nevertheless, despite the gains that have been made, girls and women continue to face gender stereotyping, sex bias, and sex discrimination.

According to the U.S. Bureau of Labor Statistics, 44% of the American work force is female, and 62% of working-age women are employed (Bolles 1986). However, traditionally female occupations, teaching and nursing, for example, tend to pay at least 20% less than traditionally male occupations. Women remain under-represented in high status occupations and executive positions. In 1983 women represented 99% of all secretaries, 82% of all elementary school teachers, 81% of all clerical workers, and 60% of all employees in the human service sector. But they represented only 32.4% of all jobs in management and executive positions, 15.8% of all physicians, 15.3% of all lawyers, and 5.8% of all engineers.

Those women who do enter high status professions tend to achieve less, as measured by both product (for instance, published work) and recognition (awards, *Who's Who* listings) than their male colleagues. The continuing underachievement of exceptionally capable women parallels a pervasive pattern of underachievement among exceptionally capable girls.

As a group, gifted girls have distinct needs that are sometimes quite different than those of their male peers. Unfortunately, educators have been slow to recognize those needs. In order to achieve their potential, gifted girls

41

must surmount the obstacles society puts in their way. In this chapter we examine some of those obstacles and consider strategies for overcoming them.

Factors Contributing to Underachievement

Underachievement is the discrepancy between performance and ability. Most often underachievement is discussed in terms of performance in school, but the concept is equally relevant to career performance. While boys may underachieve more often in school, underachievement in careers is more common among women. There are a variety of factors that contribute to a pattern of underachievement in gifted girls and women.

First, from birth both boys and girls are surrounded by gender stereotyping. Television, a pervasive purveyor of sexist imagery, is a central fixture in the lives of most children. The average American five-year-old has already watched 5,000 hours of television before starting school (Trelease 1985). However, gender stereotyping is not the exclusive domain of the electronic media. When children enter school they are likely to be confronted with stereotyping in the curriculum and by teachers.

In addition to gender stereotyping in the media, girls are far more likely to know men in executive and professional positions than they are to know women working in high status fields. If a girl has parents with equivalent educations, odds are that her father will earn significantly more than her mother. Without high achieving female role models in their lives, many gifted girls will not aspire to high status careers in which they have the ability to succeed.

A third factor is the conflicting expectations society imposes on gifted girls. Because they are gifted, there is an expectation that they will be successful in high status occupations, which require them to be assertive, aggressive, and hard working. But because they are girls, there is an expectation that they will be passive, nurturing, and altruistic. When they marry, it is assumed they will become the household manager and primary caregiver of children and defer to their husbands' career ambitions (Schwartz 1980). Even the most gifted of women would find these expectations difficult to reconcile.

A fourth factor is the peer pressure on gifted girls to underplay their academic ability. This is particularly applicable among adolescent girls in co-educational environments, where they feel they will be unpopular if they reveal their high academic ability. Also, gifted girls who express an interest in nontraditional careers or male-dominated activities may receive peer criticism or ridicule.

School: An Inhospitable Place for Gifted Girls

There is a growing body of research that indicates that the school is not a nurturing environment for gifted girls. Carol Shakeshaft (1986) argues that the structure of schools, instructional methods, and teacher-student interactions are biased toward male rather than female needs. The work of Myra Sadker and David Sadker (1986) indicates that girls, be they kindergartners or college students, constitute an underclass in our schools, receiving less teacher attention and fewer speaking opportunities than their male classmates. In their study of teacher-student interactions in classrooms at every grade level and in urban, suburban, and rural communities, they found that male students were far more likely than female students to receive the attention of the teacher and were given more opportunities to speak than their female classmates. The research of Carol Gilligan (1982) indicates that girls work more effectively in cooperative rather than competitive environments. Yet competition remains a dominant instructional mode in most classrooms.

Strategies for Nurturing Gifted Girls in the Classroom

1. De-emphasize competition. Use more cooperative and team approaches.
2. Examine teacher-student interaction patterns for gender bias. Are there differences in the way teachers relate to male and female students?
3. Be alert to examples of sexism in the textbooks. When they occur, they should be pointed out to students and discussed in class. Make sure women's history is integrated throughout your history curriculum. Supplement texts with biographies of pioneering women and social histories by women. In English classes make certain the reading list includes representative works of women writers.
4. In math and science classes discuss both historical and recent achievements of women working in those fields. Emphasize to girls the importance of continuing their math and science education.
5. Invite women in nontraditional careers to visit class. Ask them to discuss obstacles they have faced in both their formal educations and careers.
6. Avoid sexist language in the classroom.
7. Make parents of gifted girls aware of some of the obstacles they face in achieving their full potential. In parent conferences suggest ways of overcoming those obstacles. Provide parents with bibliog-

raphies of books and other references dealing with women's achievements.

8. When advising gifted girls about college choices, discuss the benefits of women's colleges. While only one-third of women from coed colleges go on to earn advanced degrees, half of the women from women's colleges go on to earn graduate degrees (*Time Magazine*, 5 October 1987). Women's colleges offer strong female role models. Women have more opportunities for leadership positions and are more likely to pursue nontraditional careers.

9. Actively recruit girls for Advanced Placement and honors classes as well as for nontraditional extracurricular activities. Girls may be more receptive to participating in nontraditional extracurricular activities if two or three are invited to join.

Strategies for School Districts Seeking to Nurture Gifted Girls

1. Offer inservice training to make staff sensitive to sex-bias in the classroom.
2. Make an effort to recruit women for staff openings in math and science. Girls (and boys) need to see strong role models in these male-dominated areas.
3. Make certain the school counseling staff are aware of factors contributing to female underachievement and are informed about strategies for counteracting these factors.

The underachievement of gifted girls and women is a loss for both the individuals involved and for society in general. By addressing those factors that contribute to underachievement, educators can nuture the talents of gifted girls and help them make contributions to society that are commensurate with their abilities.

References

Benbow, C., and Stanley. J. "Intellectually Talented Boys and Girls: Educational Profiles." *Gifted Child Quarterly* 26, no. 2 (1982): 82-88.

Blocksom, R.H. "On Plato and Gifted Girls." *Council for the Gifted Journal* 5 (1986).

Bolles, T. "Epilogue: The Progress of Women, So Far, in the Workplace." In *What Color Is Your Parachute?* Berkeley, Calif.: Ten Speed Press, 1986.

Campbell, P.B. "What's a Nice Girl Like You Doing in a Math Class?" *Phi Delta Kappan* 67 (March 1986): 516-20.

Carpenter, H. *The Inklings: C.S. Lewis, J.R.R. Tolkien, Charles Williams and Their Friends*. London: George Allen and Unwin, 1978.

Eby, J.W., and Smutny, J.F. *A Thoughtful Overview of Gifted Education*. White Plains, N.Y.: Longman, 1990.

Gilligan, C. *In a Different Voice*. Cambridge, Mass.: Harvard University Press, 1982.

Harvey, G. "Finding Reality Among the Myths: Why What You Thought About Sex Equity in Education Isn't So." *Phi Delta Kappan* 67 (March 1986): 509-12.

Hollinger, C., and Fleming, E. "Internal Barriers to the Realization of Potential: Correlates and Interrelationships Among Gifted and Talented Female Adolescents." *Gifted Child Quarterly* 28, no. 3 (1984): 135-39.

Kerr, B. *Smart Girls, Gifted Women*. Columbus: Ohio Psychology Publishing, 1985.

Kerr, B. "Smart Girls, Gifted Women: Special Guidance Concerns." *Roeper Review* 8, no.1 (1985): 30-33.

Reis, S. "We Can't Change What We Don't Recognize: Understanding the Special Needs of Gifted Females." *Gifted Child Quarterly* 31, no. 2 (1987): 83-89.

Rimm, S.B. *Underachievement Syndrome: Causes and Cures*. Watertown, Wisc.: Apple Publishing, 1986.

Sadker, M., and Sadker, D. "Sexism in the Classroom: From Grade School to Graduate School." *Phi Delta Kappan* 67 (March 1986): 512 15.

Schwartz, L. "Advocacy for the Neglected Gifted: Females." *Gifted Child Quarterly* 24, no. 3 (1980): 113-17.

Shakeshaft, C. "A Gender at Risk." *Phi Delta Kappan* 67 (March 1986): 499-503.

Time Magazine, 5 October 1987, pp. 75-76.

Trelease, J. *The Read-Aloud Handbook*. New York: Penguin, 1985.

CHAPTER SEVEN
Serving Special Populations
of the Gifted

This chapter examines two frequently neglected subgroups of the gifted, the underachieving gifted and the handicapped gifted. Each group has needs that often are unmet in traditional programs for the gifted. Underachieving gifted students have problems with motivation and self-esteem. With handicapped gifted students, their auditory, visual, and motor impairments or learning disabilities oftentimes mask their intellectual abilities.

The Underachieving Gifted

Gifted underachievers can be identified by comparing their intellectual aptitude (primarily I.Q. scores) with some measure of actual achievement, such as grades or achievement test scores. If achievement is significantly below the aptitude expectations, the student may be considered to be an underachiever.

Underachievers may exhibit a low self-concept, which often is linked to poor family relationships. They may be withdrawn or show little interest in hobbies. They may accept little responsibility for their actions and respond to adults in a hostile and rebellious manner. They are not strongly motivated toward academic achievement. Frequently gifted underachievers choose friends who share their negative attitudes toward school (Clark 1988).

The causes of underachievement are complex and varied. Whitmore (1980) cites such personality dispositions as perfectionism, hypersensitivity, and social skill deficiency as contributing to underachievement. Another factor might be the instructional style of the teacher. If a teacher focuses on basic skills with endless repetition of drill and practice, the student may soon become bored or apathetic, which is perceived as underachievement. A punitive social climate created by classroom peers may exacerbate underachievement.

In *Underachievement Syndrome: Causes and Cures*, Sylvia Rimm (1986) points out that there is no simple explanation for curing underachievement syndrome and warns that approaches that work with high achieving students may not be appropriate for the underachiever. But she does suggest that if parents and teachers adjust home and school environments in ways that nurture achievement, significant progress can be made.

Rimm goes on to identify specific instructional styles that are detrimental to underachieving students. In loosely organized classrooms, there may not be enough structure for students whose underachievement stems from lack of organizational skills. On the other hand, rigid teaching styles may lead to power struggles with gifted underachievers, forcing the teacher into a pattern of constant reprimands. Especially to be avoided are public criticism of a student's poor work or public comparisons with other students' work.

Suggestions for working with gifted underachievers include: valuing whatever accomplishments they make, assessing their progress regularly, providing opportunities for developing self-esteem, and creating learning environments that are open, accepting, and intellectually challenging. When underachievers have special abilities in such areas as music, art, or sports, provide opportunities for them to display their talents. Early on, parents of gifted underachievers need to be involved. In parent conferences teachers or counselors may gain insight into the causes of underachievement and suggest ways to overcome it.

Physically Handicapped Gifted Students

Gifted students with a physical disability tend to be identified first by that disability; their other attributes are often overlooked. They may be placed in a special school or class for the physically disabled and therefore be excluded from consideration for the gifted program. When the focus of the special education program is on compensating for the physical disability, these gifted students' intellectual and creative abilities are likely to be ignored.

This problem can be remedied to some extent through better coordination between the teacher of the handicapped and the gifted education teacher. The curriculum for handicapped gifted students should be jointly planned by the two teachers so that lessons can be modified to accommodate the particular handicap but include higher-order thinking and creative expression, which these students are capable of doing. It is also possible to include these students in gifted pull-out programs. Other efforts to develop awareness of the special needs of gifted handicapped students include national and state conferences on the topic, inservice training for special education teachers, and special graduate programs on the gifted handicapped.

47

Learning Disabled Gifted Students

Only recently have the learning disabled gifted been recognized as a sub-group within the gifted population. Too often these students are not identified as gifted because of skill deficiencies associated with the learning disability. For example, a teacher may identify a student as a poor reader but never notice what an exceptional thinker he or she is. In other cases, these gifted students have learned to compensate for their learning disability so that it is not readily apparent; but neither is their giftedness. According to Nancy Wingenbach (1987), cognitive characteristics that reliably distinguish gifted from nongifted learning disabled students cluster around four key abilities: communication of ideas, problem-solving skills, creative thought production, and knowledge retention.

Learning disabled gifted students require modifications in teaching styles and learning environments based on careful assessment of their specific learning disability. These include disorders in the psychological processing involved in comprehending or using spoken or written language (reading and writing development), in retention of information (short-term memory), in use of organizational skills, or any combination of these disorders. Other characteristics of learning disabled gifted students are low self-esteem, low frustration tolerance, preference for projects providing concrete learning experiences, and a dislike for basic skill remediation when it is isolated from meaningful learning (Wingenbach 1987).

In the past, remediation was the sole focus of learning disability programs. For the gifted, the program must remediate deficiencies while at the same time build on their academic, intellectual, or creative strengths. To help these students compensate for their weak organizational skills, it is often necessary to break down assignments into smaller segments with more frequent monitoring by the teacher. It may be necessary for teachers to modify their instructional style to match these students' learning styles.

For too long handicapped gifted students have been excluded from gifted programs simply because of their handicapping condition. Special education and gifted education staff must coordinate their efforts first to identify these students and then to design appropriate programming, which meets their needs as gifted students as well as their needs related to their handicapping condition.

References

Clark, B. *Growing Up Gifted.* 3rd ed. Columbus, Ohio: Charles E. Merrill, 1988.

Eisenburg, D. "Handicapped Children Can Be Gifted Too, Say Educators." *Education of the Handicapped* (December 1981).

Parker, A. "Living with Incongruity: Helping the Gifted Learning Disabled." *Mensa Bulletin* (May 1986): 17-18.

Rimm, S. *Underachievement Syndrome: Causes and Cures*. Waterdown, Wisc.: Apple Publishing, 1986.

Whitmore, J.R. "Recognizing Giftedness in Underachieving/L.D. Children." Paper presented at the Cuyahoga County Association for Children with Learning Disabilities and Lakewood Association for Gifted Children Conference, Strongsville, Ohio, 6 November 1987.

Whitmore, J.R. "Gifted Children with Handicapping Conditions: A New Frontier." *Exceptional Children* 48 (October 1981): 106-14.

Whitmore, J.R. *Giftedness, Conflict, and Underachievement*. Boston: Allyn and Bacon, 1980.

Whitmore, J.R., and Maker, C.J. *Intellectual Giftedness in Disabled Persons*. Rockville, Md.: Aspen Systems, 1985.

Wingenbach, N. "The Psychological and Social Problems of the Underachieving Gifted Child." Paper presented at the Cuyahoga County Association for Children with Learning Disabilities and Lakewood Association for Gifted Children Conference, Strongsville, Ohio, 6 November 1987.

49

CHAPTER EIGHT
Serving Gifted Minority and Disadvantaged Students

Giftedness can be found in every subculture — ethnic, racial, or social. However, a major problem for educators has been the identification of gifted students from these subcultures. The heart of the identification problem has been the prevailing narrow definition of giftedness and the long-time reliance on standardized aptitude and achievement tests to assess giftedness. In short, many minority and disadvantaged students exhibit giftedness in ways that conventional testing does not assess. Torrance (1978) cites an example of a highly artistic Mexican girl who was denied an award for an outstanding piece of work because she couldn't communicate to her principal and convince him that she was the artist who had produced the award-winning piece of artwork.

While the pioneer work of Guilford, Torrance, Bernal, Baldwin, Meeker, Witt, and others demonstrated cultural biases in traditional testing instruments, many school districts continued to rely heavily on these instruments for identifying the gifted. However, by 1973, as a result of data collected on the vast, untapped potential of gifted minority children, the official definition of gifted adopted by the U.S. Department of Education was expanded to include a wider range of talents (see Chapter One).

While this broader definition of giftedness was an impetus to change identification procedures, the work of Guilford also was influential in challenging long-established thinking about the nature of intelligence. His Structure of the Intellect Model, which established as many as 120 factors in cognitive functioning, dispelled the notion of intelligence as a single, quantifiable entity represented by an I.Q. score. Also, Torrance's (1977) research on "creative positives" presented a wide range of conceptual and improvisational abilities among non-mainstream populations that exposed the narrow definitions of intelligence and giftedness. Hence, the mainstream concept of intelligence became suspect not only because of its cultural biases but also because of its oversimplified view of human potential. With broadened definitions of giftedness, more minority and disadvantaged students, as well as a wider segment of the mainstream population, can be included in gifted education programs.

Several culture-free instruments have been developed that can be used for identifying gifted minority students. Among them are Torrance's Tests of Creative Thinking, which measure the imaginative and productive powers of children in verbal and nonverbal forms; the Spanish version of Wechsler; the IPAT Culture Fair Intelligence Test; the Abbreviated Binet for the Disadvantaged; Raven's Progressive Matrices Test; the Alpha Biographical Inventory; the BITCH (Black Intelligence Test of Cultural Homogeneity); the SOMPA (System for Multicultural Pluralistic Assessment); the SOI-LA (Structure of the Intellect — Learning Abilities); and Baldwin's Identification Matrix. Many of these instruments use a variety of approaches to measure potential from the cognitive, psychosocial, psychomotor, creative, and task-commitment domains. For example, the SOI-LA instrument uses Guilford's model to produce a profile of a child's intellectual processes. It stresses figural rather than verbal abilities. According to Gallagher (1983), this approach has been useful when working with the very young and with Asians and Native Americans.

Another approach to identifying giftedness among minority and disadvantaged children is use of theater techniques to identify creative potential (Sisk 1981). In Connecticut the "Encendienco Uno Llama" program uses a multiple-criteria process for identifying gifted bilingual students based on firsthand examination of students' work (Barstow 1987). Gay (1978) describes a plan for identifying gifted black students using individual conferences where candidates share their work through a demonstration or presentation and engage in group problem-solving activities to demonstrate organizational and leadership abilities.

Gifted Programs for Minority and Disadvantaged Students

Although development of programming for gifted minority students has not been widespread, there are several innovative programs that have used alternative identification methods and that capitalize on the cultural strengths of minority students.

Witt's (1968) Life Enrichment Activity Program involves community and home participation combined with structured learning activities that are integrated with perceptual-motor experiences. Frazier (1981) emphasizes parental involvement and counseling and suggests decision-making strategies, such as "futuring" (projecting oneself into the future), mental imagery, and guided fantasy, as a way of helping gifted minority students explore alternative careers. Torrance (1974) focuses on children's creative strengths and emphasizes using the arts as a medium for developing skills. Baldwin (1985) advocates structuring the curriculum to accommodate skill areas in which gifted minority students have deficits, while at the same time drawing on their cultural and creative strengths. Scruggs and Cohn (1983) describe the use of such an approach with a highly able Indian child enrolled in a university-based summer program for the gifted.

Project '89 is a summer gifted program in the suburban Chicago area involving culturally diverse students in grades 6 to 10 from both suburbia and the inner city. The program draws on the cultural strengths of its diverse student body to formulate curriculum goals. The program activities range from dance, musical comedy, theater, film-making, and writing, to futuristics, chemistry, meteorology, economics, computers, and advanced mathematics. The program stresses experimentation and invention in all content areas, from creating a piece of choreography to constructing a solar cooker. Bilingual students are able to excel in an environment that focuses on the application of ideas rather than the verbal rehearsal of abstractions. The cultural mix of white suburban and urban minority students provides for a rich exchange of talent and fosters mutual respect and admiration. The program offerings are varied enough so that any student, regardless of language problems, socioeconomic status, or skill deficiencies, is challenged. In fact, many minority students were more facile in improvising and responding to problems in original ways than were their more advantaged suburban counterparts.

In addition to incorporating cultural strengths into course content, most minority gifted programs have a strong community outreach component. The community can help to identify and support its able students. Programs such as Project LEAP in Connecticut, HEP-UP in Pennsylvania, Projects SEED and SEPE in California, and the New Orleans Center for Creative Arts all have made extensive use of community contact in their work with minority and disadvantaged gifted (Sisk 1981). Community members can help directors of gifted programs to locate talented children, inform them about the different talents valued by other cultures, function as counselors to gifted students, help students when a second language is involved, teach in the program if they have particular talents, and help the program to maintain contacts with students' families.

Conclusion

If gifted programs are to serve minority and disadvantaged students, they must alter their identification procedures to include an expanded view of intelligence and talent. Gifted programs for these students must draw on their cultural strengths and solicit the support of community members in order that the intellectual and creative potential of these students is fully realized.

References

Baldwin, A.Y. "Programs for the Gifted and Talented: Issues Concerning Minority Populations." In *The Gifted and Talented: Developmental Perspectives*, edited by F.D. Horowitz and M. O'Brien. Washington, D.C.: American Psychological Association, 1985.

Barstow, D. "Serve Disadvantaged and Serve All Gifted." *Gifted Child Monthly* 8, no. 10 (1987): 1-3.

Bernal, E.M. "Special Problems and Procedures for Identifying Minority Gifted Students." Paper presented at the Council for Exceptional Children Conference on the Exceptional Bilingual Child, New Orleans, 1981.

Bruch, C.B. "Assessment of Creativity in Culturally Different Children." *Gifted Child Quarterly* 19, no. 2 (1975): 164-74.

de Bernard, A.E. "Why Jose Can't Get in the Gifted Class: The Bilingual Child and Standardized Reading Tests." *Roeper Review* 8, no. 2 (1985): 80-82.

Frazier, M.M. "Minority Gifted Children." In *The Gifted Child, the Family, and the Community*, edited by Bernard S. Miller and Merle Price. New York: Walker and Company, 1981.

Gallagher, R. "Identification of Minority Gifted." *Illinois Council for the Gifted Journal* 1 (1983): 3-5.

Gay, J.E. "A Proposed Plan for Identifying Black Gifted Children." *Gifted Child Quarterly* 22, no. 3 (1978): 353-60.

Masten, W.G. "Identification of Gifted Minority Students: Past Research, Future Directions." *Roeper Review* 8, no. 2 (1985): 83-85.

Sato, I.S. "The Culturally Different Gifted Child: The Dawning of His Day?" *Exceptional Children* 4, no. 8 (1974): 572-76.

Scruggs, T.E., and Cohn, S.J. "A University-Based Summer Program for a Highly Able but Poorly Achieving Indian Child." *Gifted Child Quarterly* 27, no. 2 (1983): 90-93.

Sisk, D. "The Challenge of Educating the Gifted Among the Poor." In *Gifted Children: Challenging Their Potential — New Perspectives and Alternatives*, edited by A.H. Krame et al. New York: Trillium, 1981.

Swenson, E.V. "Teacher-Assessment of Creative Behavior in Disadvantaged Children." *Gifted Child Quarterly* 22, no. 3 (1978): 338-43.

Torrance, E.P. "Dare We Hope Again?" Paper prepared for the National Forum on Minority/Disadvantaged Gifted and Talented, United States Office of Gifted and Talented, Washington, D.C., 1978.

Torrance, E.P. *Discovery and Nurturance of Giftedness in the Culturally Different*. Reston, Va.: Council for Exceptional Children, 1977.

Torrance, E.P. "Differences Are Not Deficits." *Teachers College Record* 75, no. 4 (1974): 471-88.

Witt, G. *The Life Enrichment Activity Program: A Brief History*. Mimeographed. New Haven, Conn.: LEAP, 1968.

Witty, E.P. "Equal Educational Opportunity for Gifted Minority Group Children: Promise or Possibility?" *Gifted Child Quarterly* 22, no. 3 (1978): 344-51.

CHAPTER NINE
Gifted Programs for Secondary School Students

Developing gifted programs at the high school level presents more constraints than at the elementary school level. At most high schools the day is rigidly scheduled into 50-minute blocks; there is usually a higher student/teacher ratio; and the faculty is largely departmentalized. Even with these constraints, the high school offers some special advantages for gifted programming. They have well-equipped laboratories, larger libraries, and art and music rooms, all of which can be utilized for the gifted program. High school faculty tend to have stronger academic backgrounds in specialized fields, which can be a plus for gifted students with certain academic interests. Also, high school counseling staff have connections with nearby community colleges and universities, whose resources can be tapped for the gifted program.

Identifying Secondary School Gifted Students

Identifying gifted students at the secondary level is less controversial than at the elementary school level. Many high schools offer honors classes and special programs in graphic and performing arts, which gifted students can elect to take if qualified. Such programs, while selective, are well accepted in most communities and are not considered elitist.

It also is easier to identify the gifted at the high school level. By the time gifted students have reached this level, they have a record of achievement documented by test scores and school performance. And by this time many gifted students have developed specialized interests and carried out highly creative projects. Of course, some secondary students will have been in gifted classes in elementary school. Having all this information available makes the task of identification much easier at the secondary level than at the elementary level.

Even with readily available information, identification of students for secondary gifted programs should not be simply a matter of reviewing a student's file. Nor should participation in an elementary gifted program guarantee admission to a secondary program. In order to be comprehensive and equitable, the identification process at the secondary level should include peer, teacher, and self nominations; assessments of student performance (art portfolios, science fair projects, leadership experiences, awards in music, dance, speech, etc.) as well as new kinds of testing. At the secondary level students should be identified for a specific program. A student qualified for an accelerated and enriched history class may not be an appropriate candidate for a highly accelerated math or science program. In short, gifted high school students should not be placed in every available honors class.

Options in Secondary Gifted Programming

Several options are available for secondary gifted programs. In addition to offering varied and challenging curricula, they should provide opportunities for exploring postsecondary education and career choices. Among the options are independent study, short-term elective courses, special classes, college classes, and special schools. Each of these options is discussed below.

Independent Study Programs. In a typical independent study program, a gifted student might be scheduled for at least one period a day to pursue a particular topic or interest in some depth. Although independent study assumes a certain degree of self-direction, this does not mean there is no structure to the program or that little or no supervision is needed. Not all gifted high school students are self-directed learners. With some structure and supervision, students can develop the skills required for independent learning.

One organizational model for independent study is to group students into an independent study class. For example, an instructional team consisting of staff from the English and history departments might meet one period each day with 10 independent study students. An instructional team, drawn from different disciplines, facilitates interdisciplinary study. In this model, occasional class periods would be reserved for learning research techniques, student presentations, or roundtable discussions; but the major portion of class time would be devoted to independent research and study. A student's research topic is negotiated with the instructional team, and each student might have an individual consultation with one of the teachers for 30 minutes each week. If research topics are selected around a common theme, students will be able to support each other in their work.

A second independent study model is a tutorial in which a student meets once a week with an instructor to discuss the previous week's work and to plan for the week ahead. An advantage to this approach is that it requires less staff time. For example, a teacher might use part of one preparation period each week to meet with an independent study student. This model may be less satisfactory for gifted students who need more interaction with and feedback from peers; but for skilled independent learners who enjoy working alone, this can be a good option.

Combining the tutorial model with occasional after-school meetings provides for some student interaction. The agenda for these weekly or biweekly meetings might include instruction in research techniques, project presentations, and round-table discussions. This modified tutorial model encourages interdisciplinary study and can give students exposure to the knowledge and experience of more than one instructor. One disadvantage of this model is that it may interfere with students' participation in other after-school extracurricular activities.

Whatever model is used, it is important to formulate clear and reasonable expectations for both students and teachers involved in independent study. Among the items to be considered are: amount of time students will be expected to spend on their independent study project; whether students will negotiate a contract with their independent study advisor; criteria to be used to evaluate student work; whether written progress reports will be required of students and, if so, with what frequency; and provision for students to evaluate the quality of assistance received from their advisor.

Short-Term Elective Courses. These courses may range in length from a few weeks to several months. They give gifted students exposure to selected topics or issues not generally covered in the regular curriculum. Most often they are offered after school and are taught by instructors who are enthusiastic about their subject and have a depth of knowledge in the area. There are an endless number of topics well suited for short-term elective courses, which can be determined by faculty and student interest. Many able teachers enjoy developing a short course on a topic of their choosing when they know they will be working with gifted students.

Ideally, short-term elective courses should be offered during the regular school day. If scheduling can be arranged within the school's master schedule, gifted students can sign up for a new offering each quarter. However, given the scheduling constraints in most high schools, after-school sessions may be the only feasible option. As with independent study programs, expectations for students and teachers should be clearly delineated, including evaluation criteria, attendance requirements, and provisions for withdrawing from the course. If students are not receiving credit for the class, requirements for outside reading should be reasonable.

Special Classes. This is by far the most common model of gifted programming in secondary schools. Advanced Placement courses and honors classes fall into this category, as do many enrichment classes. The Advanced Placement (AP) program is administered by the College Entrance Examination Board. High school students taking AP courses can earn college credit if they do well on the AP examinations. The examinations are scored on a five-point scale. Most colleges and universities grant credit if students score 4 or 5, and some require only a score of 3. Students enrolled in AP courses who elect not to take the examination or who do not score high enough to earn college credit still profit from the experience of doing rigorous, college-level work.

AP examinations are available in the following areas: American History, Art History, Studio Art, Biology, Chemistry, Classics, English, European History, French Language, French Literature, German Literature, Calculus (2 levels), Music (Listening and Literature), Music Theory, Physics (2 levels), Spanish Language, and Spanish Literature. Information about this program can be obtained from the College Entrance Examination Board, Box 592, Princeton, New Jersey 08541.

Generally, AP courses fall within a single discipline. Honors classes, however, can be interdisciplinary using a team-teaching approach. For example, an American history teacher and an American literature teacher can be teamed and scheduled to teach back-to-back honors classes during the same two periods each day. As an instructional team, these teachers design an integrated literature and history course, decide how time will be allotted for various units, and organize groups of students for special projects.

With larger blocks of time and flexible grouping, these interdisciplinary courses give gifted students both depth and breadth in content areas, which they are not likely to experience in regular courses. However, honors classes run the risk of being simply more-of-the-same, differing only in the pace of instruction and the quantity of homework required. According to Reis and Renzulli (1986), there is a tendency for advanced courses to require students to cover too much material in too little time, with few opportunities for the in-depth study of self-selected topics. They go on to warn that selection of instructors to teach honors classes should not be used as a reward for long and loyal service but rather should be based on subject matter competence and skill in working with gifted secondary students.

Because many bright students have learned from their earlier school experiences that they can make top grades with little effort, the more challenging environment of honors classes can be a shock at first. A rocky start should not be grounds for dismissal from an honors program. Rather, students who are having trouble should be given help with managing their time and developing better study habits.

Enrollment in College Classes. In communities across the country, exceptionally able high school students can now attend classes at nearby community colleges and four-year institutions (Greenberg 1989). These concurrent enrollment programs allow students to earn their high school diploma credits and college credits at the same time. Such programs are fairly easy to implement if there is a college within commuting distance. Students are released from their high schools to take a college class during the school day, or they can enroll in late afternoon or evening classes. Many juniors or seniors are eager to get a head start on their college careers and enjoy the status of being in a college class with older students. Others may be fully capable of college-level work but are socially immature and would not be comfortable in the college setting. Teachers and counselors have an important role in determining whether a student has the maturity to take college-level classes.

High school students involved in college programs should not be left to shift entirely for themselves. In some schools, one staff member is responsible for monitoring the progress of students taking classes off campus. In other schools, a faculty member is assigned counseling responsibilities for students taking courses in that faculty member's academic area.

Special Schools. Many special schools have been established for the gifted and talented. One of the oldest and best known is the High School of Performing Arts in New York City. Many special schools have a particular emphasis, such as math, science, or the performing arts; but they also provide a good general education. Most are operated by school districts, a few are private, and a growing number are state-sponsored residential schools. Admission to these schools is highly competitive, and their staffs are carefully recruited for their ability to work with gifted and talented adolescents.

A variation of the special school for the gifted is the school-within-a-school organizational plan. This model is used in some large, comprehensive high schools to divide the student body into more cohesive groups with a separate faculty in each school serving a smaller number of students. With this organizational model, scheduling, curriculum, and physical facilities can be tailored to serve the special needs of gifted students. At the same time, this model allows gifted students to draw on all the resources of a large high school.

Special Competitions and Academic Teams

A variety of special competitions provide gifted secondary students with intellectual challenges, peer interaction, and even travel opportunities. The Future Problem Solving Bowl developed by E. Paul Torrance has an advanced division for students in grades 10 through 12. The focus is on problems in business and government. Teams compete nationally and their proposals are forwarded to cooperating businesses or agencies for review and ranking (Crabbe 1985). For further information, contact Future Problem Solving Program, 115 Main Street, Aberdeen, NC 28315.

Another special competition is the Odyssey of the Mind (OM) Program, formerly known as Olympics of the Mind. This program began in 1978 but had to change its name in 1984 when the U.S. Olympic Committee denied it permission to use the word "Olympics." This national program involves approximately 40,000 students, K-12, each year, with Division III serving secondary school students. For further information, contact: OM Association, P.O. Box 27, Glassboro, NJ 08028.

Conclusion

Although the traditional structure of American high schools can make it difficult to implement special programs for the gifted, there are options within existing organizational structures to provide advanced or accelerated programs for the gifted, such as honors classes or AP courses. The other options described in this chapter require both leadership and cooperative effort to implement, but they are certainly worth pursuing. Some of that leadership can be found in the gifted students themselves, who should be involved in the planning, implementation, and evaluation of gifted programming.

References

Cline, S. *The Independent Learner: A Guide to Creative Independent Study*. East Aurora, N.Y.: D.O.K., 1986.

Cox, J.; Daniel, N.; and Boston, B. *Educating Able Learners: Programs and Promising Practices*. Austin: University of Texas Press, 1985.

Crabbe, A. "Future Problem Solving." In *Developing Minds: A Resource Book for Teaching Thinking*, edited by A. Costa. Fairfax, Va.: Association for Supervision and Curriculum Development, 1985.

Gallagher, J. *Teaching the Gifted Child*. Boston: Allyn and Bacon, 1985.

Greenberg, A.R. *Concurrent Enrollment Programs: College Credit for High School Students*. Fastback 284. Bloomington, Ind.: Phi Delta Kappa Educational Foundation, 1989.

Keating, D.P. "Secondary School Programs." In *The Gifted and Talented*, edited by A.H. Passow. Chicago: University of Chicago Press, 1979.

Maker, C. *Curriculum Development for the Gifted*. Rockville, Md.: Aspen Systems, 1982.

Perry, P. *Full Flowering: A Parent and Teacher Guide to Programs for the Gifted*. Columbus: Ohio Psychology Publishing, 1985.

Reis, S., and Renzulli, J. "The Secondary Triad Model." In *Systems and Models for Developing Programs for the Gifted and Talented*, edited by S. Reis and J. Renzulli. Mansfield Center, Conn.: Creative Learning Press, 1986.

Whitlock, B.W. *Don't Hold Them Back: A Critique and Guide to New High School-College Articulation Models*. New York: College Entrance Exam Board, 1978.

Zimmerman, W., and Brody, L. "Part-Time College Gifted High School Students." *Gifted Child Today* (March/April 1986).

CHAPTER TEN
Evaluating Gifted Programs

Accountability has become a watchword in education today. School boards, legislators, parents, and the tax-paying public want to know — and have a right to know — if special school programs are delivering what they promised, and this includes programs for the gifted. However, there are a number of problems in evaluating gifted programs. Because gifted education is the "new kid on the block" in many school districts, there is no experience in evaluating such programs compared, say, to the reading program. Many of the objectives of the gifted program cannot be easily quantified, and standardized tests are seldom appropriate for assessing the goals of gifted education. Also, because the amount of time children typically spend in the gifted program is limited, it is difficult to distinguish outcomes attributed to the gifted program from those of the regular program. Finally, most gifted education programs today operate on a shoestring budget with little or no funds to spend on evaluation.

Despite the problems, those who direct gifted programs and fail to provide for evaluation put themselves at risk. Dettmer (1985) explains why: "Because gifted programs are not popular and probably never will be, they must be defended and promoted by solid evidence of gifted student growth, cost effectiveness of the program and positive ripple effects for all students throughout the school system" (p. 146).

Need for Clear Objectives

Evaluation is meaningless, if not impossible, when programs have poorly defined objectives. An evaluation plan must be formulated at the start-up phase of a gifted program. As Dettmer (1985) states, "The design of an evaluation process is a powerful device for forcing clarification of program goals. In fact, it reveals the program goals or the nonexistence of authentic goals" (p. 147). A goal statement such as "Students will become more creative" is too vague because it does not indicate how creativity will be expressed. A better-stated goal might be: "Students will engage in projects or create products that reflect original thinking and creative expression." Evaluating this goal becomes possible when students have completed their projects or products, which then can be assessed by their teachers and peers.

When planning for evaluation, Clark (1988) suggests the initial questions should be: Who needs to know what? What persons are involved in or responsible for the gifted program and what do these persons need or expect to know from an evaluation? A comprehensive evaluation plan should include assessment of students' academic progress, social growth, decision-making skills, and leadership abilities. In addition, the plan should assess teacher effectiveness and program effectiveness.

Student Evaluation

With the emphasis on critical thinking and creative expression in gifted education, student evaluation should be targeted on student products. This can best be done by collecting individual portfolios of students' work. These portfolios might include art work, research papers or original writing done in an English class, science projects, mathematical proofs, or even student-designed computer programs. Student products collected over a period of time, when evaluated with a set of established criteria, provide a record of growth and achievement.

Michael Scriven (1980), proponent of client-centered evaluation, advocates that evaluation also include "soft" data. Questions for collecting soft data at the elementary school level might be: In what ways did you grow during the program? List any new experiences, activities, and perspectives. What did you like best? Least? What would you like to see changed or improved in the program? As a result of being in the class, are you able to think more analytically? More creatively? Please give specific examples.

For older students, soft data questions might be: If you could restructure this course to make it better, what would you do? What were the strengths of the course that you would not change? Were the atmosphere, schedule, and facilities conducive to learning? How was it different from other classes you have attended? Comment on specifics of the curriculum (reading, lecture, discussion) that you felt were either too easy, too hard, inappropriate, or exemplary? Comment on the ability of your instructor. Has the class given you ideas or directions about your future work? Comment on the evaluation/grading in this course. Is it a fair system? How would you change it? Do you feel that you have grown during the class in terms of awareness of new ideas and involvement in new experiences? As a result of being in the class, are you able to think more analytically? More creatively? Please give specific examples.

Parents also should be included in client-centered evaluation. Here are some questions to ask parents: Does your child talk to you about the program? Do you favor continuation of this program? Why or why not? Do you favor the establishment of additional gifted programs? What changes would you like to see in this program? Comment on the fairness of selection of students for this program. Were you satisfied with the counseling and communication from the teachers and administrators in the program? Comment on how this class does or does not relate to your child's future education plans or career goals.

These kinds of soft data go beyond evaluation of student products. They offer a more complete picture of the students' total experience in the gifted program, and they provide a means for parents' feedback. The open-endedness of the questions allows for the airing of issues and ideas that may have never occurred to the evaluator.

Teacher and Program Evaluation

Cronbach (1982) advocates practitioner-centered evaluation and points out that evaluation that does not involve those who deliver the services is usually ignored. Teachers of the gifted can evaluate themselves and their programs on an informal basis whenever they read articles, attend seminars and conferences, or visit other programs. By comparing their program with different models, by making notes on the strengths and weaknesses of different programs as well as the feasibility of adapting promising ideas, teachers can make modifications in their own programs. Through these informal evaluations, programs can be improved gradually.

Formal teacher evaluations also are important. An evaluation questionnaire for teachers might include the following questions: Please identify what you perceive to be the strongest aspects of this program. What do you perceive to be the program's weaknesses? List any changes you would make in this program. Comment on whether or not this program should be continued next year. Indicate whether the inservice training you received was helpful? How could it be improved? Comment on selection of students for the program. Could the selection process be improved? How? How could the curriculum be improved? How could the schedule and classroom environment be improved? How could evaluation and grading of students be improved?

Staff meetings are also a time when the faculty can do program evaluation. Such meetings provide a structured setting in which the staff can share and discuss ideas and concerns among themselves and with administrators. Staff meetings prior to starting the gifted program can be used to communicate program goals. After the program is under way, staff meetings help the gifted faculty to solidify their roles in the program and to maintain open communication.

A Five-Year Evaluation Plan

There are too many elements in a gifted program to attempt to evaluate each of them every year. A better approach is to break down the various elements and evaluate them over a five-year period. Eby and Smutny (1990) offer a five-year evaluation plan in which year one focuses on philosophy and definition issues (talent areas to be served, definition of giftedness or talent in each area). Year two focuses on gifted identification issues (numbers to be served in each talent area, numbers to be served at each grade level, levels of ability or talent required for admission, review of criteria for selection, review of instruments and other procedures used for identification). Year three focuses on evaluation of services (types, quantity, quality, variety, costs). Year four focuses on curriculum and instructional issues (acceleration, enrichment, independent study, curriculum areas, goals and objectives, and appropriateness of instructional strategies). Year five focuses on evaluating effects or impact of the program for each talent area served.

Of course, many of the issues are interrelated. The philosophy, objectives, and the identification issues may need to be refined and re-evaluated each year. Unexpected events such as loss of funding, community pressures, and staff turnover may require adjustments in the evaluation plan. But if a plan is in place, it should be able to accommodate changing conditions.

Conclusion

The gifted education scene is in constant flux. New federal and state guidelines, new sources of funding, new program models, and the movement for increasing parent involvement all influence gifted education. By having an on-going evaluation process, educators can ensure that their gifted programs are sensitive to these changes and that they can react to these changes to strengthen their programs and keep on the cutting edge.

References

Callahan, C. "Issues in Evaluating Programs for the Gifted." *Gifted Child Quarterly* 27, no. 1 (1983): 3-7.

Carter, K.R. "Evaluation Design. Issues Confronting Evaluators of Gifted Programs." *Gifted Child Quarterly* 30, no. 2 (1986): 88-92.

Carter, K.R., and Hamilton, W. "Formulative Evaluation of Gifted Programs: A Process and Model." *Gifted Child Quarterly* 29, no. 1 (1985): 5-11.

Clark, B. *Growing Up Gifted*. 3rd ed. Columbus, Ohio: Charles E. Merrill, 1988.

Cronbach, L. *Designing Evaluations of Educational and Social Programs*. San Francisco: Jossey-Bass, 1982.

Dettmer, P. "Gifted Program Scope, Structure and Evaluation." *Roeper Review* 7, no. 3 (1985): 146-52.

Eby, J.W., and Smutny, J.F. *A Thoughtful Overview of Gifted Education*. White Plains, N.Y.: Longman, 1990.

Gallagher, J. *Teaching the Gifted Child*. Boston: Allyn and Bacon, 1985.

Scriven, M. *The Logic of Evaluation*. Inverness, Calif.: Edgepress, 1980.

Whitmore, J. *Giftedness, Conflict, and Underachievement*. Boston: Allyn and Bacon, 1980.

A Gifted
Education Bibliography

Abraham, Willard. *Common Sense About Gifted Children*. New York: Harper & Row, 1958.

American Association for Gifted Children. *Reaching Out: Advocacy for the Gifted and Talented*. New York: Teachers College Press, 1980.

Balsame, K.L. *Exploring the Lives of Gifted People in the Arts and Sciences*. Carthage, Ill.: Good Apple, 1987.

Barbe, W., and Renzulli, J., eds. *Psychology and Education of the Gifted*. 2nd ed. New York: Irvington, 1975.

Beck, J. *How to Raise a Brighter Child*. New York: Trident, 1967.

Betts, B.T. *Autonomous Learner Model for the Gifted and Talented*. Greeley, Colo.: Autonomous Learning Publications, 1985.

Biondi, A.M. *The Creative Process*. Buffalo, N.Y.: D.O.K., 1972.

Bloom, B. *Taxonomy of Educational Objectives. Handbook I: Cognitive Domain*. New York: David McKay, 1956.

Bloom, B.S. "The Role of Gifts and Markers in the Development of Talent." *Exceptional Children* 48, no. 6 (1982): 510-22.

Bloom, B.S., ed. *Developing Talent in Young People*. New York: Ballantine, 1985.

Boston, B., ed. *Gifted and Talented: Developing Elementary and Secondary School Programs*. Reston, Va.: Council for Exceptional Children, 1975.

Brooks, P. *A Teacher's Guide for Project STEP: Strategies for Targeting Early Potential*. Prince George's County, Md.: Prince George's County Public School System, 1984.

Bruner, J. *The Process of Education*. Cambridge, Mass.: Harvard University Press, 1960.

Bruner, J.S. *Beyond the Information Given*. New York: Norton, 1973.

Canfield, J., and Wells, H. *200 Ways to Enhance Self-Concept in the Classroom*. Englewood Cliffs, N.J.: Prentice-Hall, 1976.

Clark, B. *Growing Up Gifted*, 3rd ed. Columbus, Ohio: Charles E. Merrill, 1988.

Clark, B. *Optimizing Learning: The Integrative Model in the Classroom*. Columbus, Ohio: Charles E. Merrill, 1986.

Clark, B., and Kaplan, S. *Improving Differentiated Curricula for the Gifted/Talented*. Los Angeles: California Association for the Gifted, 1981.

Cohen, L.M. "Infants' Interests: Seeds of Creative Development." *Illinois Journal for the Gifted* 7 (1988): 32-36.

Cohen, L.M. "13 Tips for Teaching Gifted Children." *Teaching Exceptional Children* 20, no.1 (1987): 34-38.

Cohen, L.M., and Kamihira, K. "Look Out World." *Gifted Child Today* 10, no. 4 (1987): 51-53.

Colangelo, N., and Lafrenz, N. "Counseling the Culturally Diverse Gifted." *Gifted Child Quarterly* 25, no. 1 (1981): 27-30.

Costa, A.L., ed. *Developing Minds: A Resource Book for Teaching Thinking.* Alexandria, Va.: Association for Supervision and Curriculum Development, 1985.

Costa, A.L. "Mediating the Metacognitive." *Educational Leadership* 42, no. 3 (1984): 57-62.

Covington, M.; Crutchfield, R.S.; Olten, R.; and Davies, L. *Productive Thinking Program.* Columbus, Ohio: Charles E. Merrill, 1972.

Cox, J.; Daniel, N.; and Boston, B. *Educating Able Learners.* Austin: University of Texas Press, 1985.

Daniels, P. *Teaching the Gifted/Learning Disabled Child.* Rockville, Md.: Aspen, 1983.

Davis, G., and Rimm, S. *Education of the Gifted and Talented.* Englewood Cliffs, N.J.: Prentice-Hall, 1985.

deBernard, A. "Gifted Minority Students: Why Jose Can't Get in the Gifted Class: The Bilingual Child and Standardized Reading Tests." *Roeper Review* 8 (November 1985).

de Bono, E. "The Direct Teaching of Thinking as a Skill." *Phi Delta Kappan* 64 (June 1983): 703-708.

Delp, J., and Martinson, R. *The Gifted and Handicapped: A Handbook for Parents.* Ventura, Calif.: NS/LTI/GT, 1975.

Delp, J., and Martinson, R. *The Gifted and Talented: A Handbook for Parents.* Reston, Va.: Council for Exceptional Children, 1974.

Dickinson, R. *Caring for the Gifted.* North Quincy, Mass.: Christopher, 1970.

Eberle, R. F. "Developing Imagination Through Scamper." In *Guide to Creative Action*, edited by S.J. Parnes, R.B. Noller, and A.M. Biondi. New York: Scribners, 1977.

Eberle, R.F. *Scamper: Games for Imagination Development.* East Aurora, N.Y.: D.O.K., 1971.

Eby, J. *Eby Gifted Behavior Index.* East Aurora, N.Y.: D.O.K., 1988.

Eby, J. "Developing Gifted Behavior." *Educational Leadership* (April 1984): 35-43.

Eby, J. "Gifted Behavior: A Non-Elitist Approach." *Educational Leadership* (May 1983): 30-36.

Eby, J.W., and Smutny, J.F. *A Thoughtful Overview of Gifted Education.* White Plains, N.Y.: Longman, 1990.

Elkind, D. *Child Development and Education: A Piagetian Perspective.* New York: Oxford University Press, 1976.

Feldhusen, J.F., and Treffinger, D.J. *Creative Thinking and Problem Solving in Gifted Education*. Dubuque, Iowa: Kendall Hunt, 1980.

Feldhusen, J.F.; Treffinger, D.J.; and Pine, P. *Teaching Children How to Think*. Teacher's ed. Technical Report No. NIE-G-74-0063. Washington, D.C.: National Institute of Education, 1975.

Feldhusen, J.F.; VanTassel-Baska, J.; and Seeley, K. *Excellence in Educating the Gifted*. Denver, Colo.: Love, 1989.

Feldman, D. *Nature's Gambit: Child Prodigies and the Development of Human Potential*. New York: Basic Books, 1986.

Feldman, D.H. *Develomental Approaches to Giftedness and Creativity: New Directions for Child Development*. San Francisco: Jossey-Bass, 1982.

Feuerstein, R. *Instrumental Enrichment*. Baltimore, Md.: University Park Press, 1980.

Feuerstein, R. *Learning Potential Assessment Device*. Baltimore, Md.: University Park Press, 1978.

Fine, B. *Underachievers: How They Can Be Helped*. New York: E.P. Dutton, 1967.

Fox, L.H., and Durden, W.G. *Educating Verbally Gifted Youth*. Fastback 176. Bloomington, Ind.: Phi Delta Kappa Educational Foundation, 1982.

Galbraith, J. *The Gifted Kid's Survival Guide (For Ages Ten and Under)*. Minneapolis, Minn.: Free Spirit Publishing, 1984.

Gallagher, J.J. *Teaching the Gifted Child*. 3rd ed. Boston: Allyn and Bacon, 1985.

Gardner, H. *Frames of Mind: The Theory of Multiple Intelligences*. New York: Basic Books, 1983.

Gardner, J.W. *Excellence*. New York: W.W. Norton, 1984.

Gardner, J.W. *Excellence: Can We Be Equal and Excellent Too?* New York: Harper & Row, 1961.

Guilford, J.P. *Creative Talents: Their Nature, Use, and Development*. Buffalo, N.Y.: Bearly, 1986.

Guilford, J.P. *The Nature of Human Intelligence*. New York: McGraw-Hill, 1967.

Halsted, J. *Guiding Gifted Readers from Preschool to High School*. Columbus: Ohio Psychology Publishing, 1988.

Hoard, E. *Getting Kids Ready to Take on the World*. Phoenix, Ariz.: Kathy Kolbe Concept, 1983.

Horowitz, F., and O'Brien, M. *The Gifted and Talented: Developmental Perspectives*. Columbus: Ohio Psychology Publishing, 1985.

Johnson, N.L. *Questioning Makes the Difference*. Videotape. Dayton, Ohio: Creative Learning Consultants, 1990.

Joyce, B., and Weil, M. *Models of Teaching*. Englewood Cliffs, N.J.: Prentice-Hall, 1986.

Kaplan, S.N. *Providing Programs for the Gifted and Talented: A Handbook*. Ventura County, Calif.: Office of the Ventura County Superintendent of Schools, 1974.

Karnes, M. *The Underserved: Our Gifted Young Children.* Reston, Va.: Council for Exceptional Children, 1983.

Karnes, M. "Young Handicapped Children Can Be Gifted and Talented." *Journal for the Education of the Gifted* 2, no. 3 (1979): 157-72.

Kerr, B.A. *Smart Girls, Gifted Women.* Columbus: Ohio Psychology Publishing, 1985.

Khatena, J. "Training Preschool Children to Think Creatively with Pictures." *Journal of Educational Psychology* 62 (1970): 384-86.

Kitano, M. "Ethnography of a Preschool for the Gifted: What Gifted Young Children Actually Do." *Gifted Child Quarterly* 29, no. 2 (1985): 67-71.

Kitano, M. "Issues and Problems in Establishing Preschool Programs for Gifted." *Roeper Review* 7, no. 4 (1985): 212-13.

Kitano, M. "Young Gifted Children: Strategies for Preschool Teachers." *Young Children* (May 1982): 14-22.

Kitano, M., and Kirby, D. *Gifted Education: A Comprehensive View.* Boston: Little, Brown, 1986.

Kohlberg, L. *Collected Papers on Moral Development and Moral Education.* Cambridge, Mass.: Moral Education and Research Foundation, 1973.

Maker, C.J. *Teaching Models in Education of the Gifted.* Rockville, Md.: Aspen, 1982.

Martinson, R. *The Identification of the Gifted and Talented.* Ventura, Calif.: Office of the Ventura County Superintendent of Schools, 1974.

Maslow, A. *Motivation and Personality.* Rev. ed. New York: Harper & Row, 1970.

Meeker, M. *The Structure of Intellect: Its Use and Interpretation.* Columbus, Ohio: Charles E. Merrill, 1969.

Moore, E.W.; McCann, H.; and McCann, J. *Creative and Critical Thinking.* 2nd ed. Boston: Houghton Mifflin, 1985.

Myers, R.E., and Torrance, E.P. *Invitations to Thinking and Doing.* Lexington, Mass.: Ginn, 1964.

Osborn, A. *Applied Imagination.* New York: Scribner's, 1963.

Parker, J.P. *Instructional Strategies for Teaching the Gifted.* Boston: Allyn and Bacon, 1989.

Parnes, S.J. *The Magic of Your Mind.* Buffalo, N.Y.: Bearly, 1981.

Parnes, S.J. *Creativity: Unlocking Human Potential.* East Aurora, N.Y.: D.O.K., 1972.

Passow, A.H. *Education for Gifted Children and Youth: An Old Issue — A New Challenge.* Ventura, Calif.: Office of the Ventura County Superintendent of Schools, 1980.

Perkins, D.N. *The Mind's Best Work.* Cambridge, Mass.: Harvard University Press, 1981.

Perrone, P., and Male, R. *Developmental Education and Guidance of Talented Learners.* Rockville, Md.: Aspen, 1981.

Perry, P. *Full Flowering: A Parent and Teacher Guide to Programs for the Gifted.* Columbus: Ohio Psychology Publishing, 1985.

Piaget, J. "Development and Learning." In *Piaget Rediscovered*, edited by R.E. Ripple and V.N. Rockcastle. Ithaca, N.Y.: Cornell University Press, 1964.

Rawlinson, J.G. *Creative Thinking and Brainstorming*. New York: John Wiley & Sons, 1981.

Renzulli, J., ed. *Systems and Models for Developing Programs for the Gifted and Talented*. Mansfield Center, Conn.: Creative Learning Press, 1986.

Renzulli, J.S. *What Makes Giftedness?* Ventura County, Calif.: Office of the Ventura County Superintendent of Schools, 1979.

Renzulli, J. *The Enrichment Triad Model: A Guide for Developing Defensible Programs for the Gifted*. Wethersfield, Conn.: Creative Learning Press, 1977.

Renzulli, J. *New Directions in Creativity*. New York: Harper & Row, 1973.

Renzulli, J.; Smith, L.; and Reis, S. "Curriculum Compacting: An Essential Strategy for Working with Gifted Students." *Elementary School Journal* 82, no. 3 (1982): 185-94.

Rimm, S. *How to Parent so Children Will Learn*. Columbus: Ohio Psychology Publishing, 1990.

Rimm, S. *Underachievement Syndrome: Causes and Cures*. Watertown, Wisc.: Apple Publishing, 1986.

Roedell, W.; Jackson, N.E.; and Robinson, H.R. *Gifted Young Children*. New York: Teachers College Press, 1980.

Sisk, D. *Creative Teaching of the Gifted*. New York: McGraw-Hill, 1987.

Sisk, D. "Gifted Education: A Global Phenomenon." *Gifted Children Monthly* 7, no. 9 (1986): 102.

Sisk, D. "Communication Skills for the Gifted." *Gifted Child Quarterly* 19 (1975): 66-68.

Smith, J.C. *Beginning Early: Adult Responsibilities to Gifted Young Children*. New York: Trillium, 1986.

Smutny, J.; Veenker, K.; and Veenker, S. *Your Gifted Child: How to Recognize and Develop the Special Talents in Your Child from Birth to Age Seven*. New York: Facts on File, 1989.

Stanley, J. *The Gifted and the Creative: A Fifty-Year Perspective*. Baltimore, Md.: Johns Hopkins University Press, 1977.

Stanley, J.C., and Benbow, C.P., eds. *Academic Precocity: Aspects of Its Development, Consequences, and Nurturance*. Baltimore, Md.: Johns Hopkins University Press, 1983.

Stanley, J.C.; Keating, D.P.; and Fox, L.H., eds. *Mathematical Talent: Discovery, Description and Development*. Baltimore, Md.: Johns Hopkins University Press, 1974.

Tannenbaum, A.J. *Gifted Children: Psychological and Educational Perspectives*. New York: Macmillan, 1983.

Taylor, C.W. "Cultivating Multiple Creative Talents in Students." *Journal for the Education of the Gifted* 8, no. 3 (1985): 187-98.

Taylor, C.W. *Teaching for Talents and Gifts: 1978 Status*. Washington, D.C.: National Institute of Education, 1978.

Taylor, I.A. "An Emerging View of Creative Actions." In *Perspectives in Creativity*, edited by I.A. Taylor and J.W. Getzels. Chicago: Aldine, 1975.

Torrance, E.P. *Mentor Relationships: How They Aid Creative Achievement, Endure, Change, and Die.* Buffalo, N.Y.: Bearly, 1984.

Torrance, E.P. *Discovery and Nurturance of Giftedness in the Culturally Different.* Reston, Va.: Council for Exceptional Children, 1977.

Torrance, E.P. *Education and the Creative Potential.* Minneapolis: University of Minnesota Press, 1967.

Torrance, E.P. *Torrance Tests of Creative Thinking: Norms-Technical Manual.* Princeton, N.J.: Personnel Press, 1966.

Torrance, E.P. *Guiding Creative Talent.* Englewood Cliffs, N.J.: Prentice-Hall, 1964.

Torrance, E.P., and Myers, R.E. *Creative Learning and Teaching.* N.Y.: Harper & Row, 1970.

Torrance, E.P., and Safter, H.T. *The Incubation Model of Teaching: Getting Beyond the Aha!* Buffalo, N.Y.: Bearly, 1990.

Torrance, E.P.; Weiner, D.; Presbury, J.; and Henderson, M. *Save Tomorrow for the Children* Buffalo, N.Y.: Bearly, 1987.

Treffinger, D. "Research on Creativity." *Gifted Child Quarterly* 30, no. 1 (1986): 15-19.

Webb, J.; Meckstroth, E.; and Tolan, S. *Guiding the Gifted Child: A Practical Source for Parents and Teachers.* Columbus: Ohio Psychology Publishing, 1989.

Weiner, D.A. *Instructional Units for Integrating Academics and Creativity: Methods and Materials in Gifted Education.* Louisville, Ky.: University of Louisville, 1985.

Whitmore, J. *Giftedness, Conflict and Underachievement.* Boston: Allyn and Bacon, 1980.

Williams, F.E. *A Total Creativity Program for Individualizing and Humanizing the Learning Process.* Englewood Cliffs, N.J.: Educational Technology Publications, 1972.

APPENDIX A
National Organizations Serving the Gifted

American Association for Gifted Children
15 Gramercy Park
New York, NY 10003

A voluntary, non-profit organization that emphasizes cooperation among community and professional groups in promoting education of the gifted.

The Gifted Child Society, Inc.
190 Rock Road
Glen Rock, NJ 07452

An advocacy group to raise public awareness about the gifted, to promote public school education for all gifted and talented children, and to encourage teacher training in gifted education.

National Association for Gifted Children
5100 N. Edgewood Drive
St. Paul, MN 55112

A professional organization primarily for educators. Publishes *Gifted Child Quarterly*.

The Association for the Gifted (TAG)
Council for Exceptional Children
1920 Association Drive
Reston, VA 22091

Non-profit organization serving gifted children. Publishes *Journal of the Education of the Gifted*.

Supporting Emotional Needs of Gifted (SENG)
Wright State University
P.O. Box 1102
Dayton, OH 45401

National center for testing and identification of gifted. Provides guidance to parents and professionals as well as consultative and educational services to educators, health-care personnel, industry leaders, and community groups.

National/State Leadership Training Institute on Gifted and Talented (NS/LTI/GT)
Ventura County Superintent of Schools
535 East Main Street
Ventura, CA 93009

A pioneer in gifted education, this county school system offers a variety of publications, publishes a newsletter, and provides consultant services.

Gifted Students Institute
P.O. Box 113881
Fort Worth, TX 76110-0388

Organization for educators and parents. Publishes *Educating Able Learners*.

World Council for Gifted and Talented Children
University of South Florida
Tampa, FL 33620

Designed to advance the development of gifted and talented children and to stimulate research on the nature of giftedness. The Council is a network of more than 50 countries. Every two years it holds an international conference on the gifted; it also offers a newsletter and a journal.

APPENDIX B
Professional Journals
on the Gifted

Educating Able Learners:
  Discovering and Nurturing Talent
Gifted Students Institute
P.O. Box 11388
Fort Worth, TX 76110-0388

Gifted Child Today
P.O. Box 6448
Mobile, AL 36660

Gifted Children Monthly
213 Hollydell Drive
Sewell, NJ 08080

Gifted Child Quarterly
Box 30-Suite 140
4175 Lovell Road
Circle Pines, MN 55014

Illinois Council for Gifted Journal
500 North Clark Drive
Palatine, IL 60067

Journal for the Education
  of the Gifted
CEC-TAG
1920 Association Drive
Reston, VA 22091

Prism Magazine
P.O. Box 030464
Ft. Lauderdale, FL 33303

Roeper Review
Roeper City and Country
  Day School
P.O. Box 329
Bloomfield Hills, MI 48013

Understanding Our Gifted
Snowpeak Publications
P.O. Box 3489
Littleton, CO 80122

APPENDIX C
Directory of State Education Departments' Gifted Education Programs

Alabama
Programs for Gifted
Alabama State Department of
  Education
868 State Office Building
Montgomery, AL 36130-3903
(205) 261-5099

Alaska
Office for Exceptional Services
Alaska Department of Education
P.O. Box F
Juneau, AK 99811
(907) 465-2970

Arizona
Gifted Programs
Arizona Department of Education
1535 West Jefferson
Phoenix, AZ 85007
(602) 255-5031

Arkansas
Programs for Gifted/Talented
Room 105C, Education Building
4 Capitol Mall
Little Rock, AR 72201
(501) 371-5437

California
Gifted and Talented Education
California State Department
  of Education
P.O. Box 944272
Sacramento, CA 95814
(916) 323-4781

Colorado
Gifted and Talented Student
  Programming
Colorado Department of Education
201 E. Colfax
Denver, CO 80204
(303) 866-6765

Connecticut
Gifted/Talented Programs
Connecticut State Department
  of Education
165 Capitol Avenue
Hartford, CT 06145
(203) 566-3695

Delaware
Programs for Gifted and Talented
Townsend Building
Delaware State Department
  of Public Instruction
P.O. Box 1402
Dover, DE 19903
(302) 736-4667

District of Columbia
Gifted and Talented Education
  Program
Bryan Elementary School
13th and Independence Ave., SE
Washington, DC 20003
(202) 724-3894

Florida
Gifted Programs
Bureau of Education of
  Exceptional Children
Knott Building
Florida Department of Education
Tallahassee, FL 32399
(904) 488-3103

Georgia
Programs for the Gifted
Georgia Department of Education
Twin Towers East, Suite 1970
Atlanta, GA 30334
(404) 656-6317

Hawaii
Gifted and Talented Program
Office of Instructional Services
189 Lunalilo Homo Road
Honolulu, HI 96425
(808) 395-9590

Idaho
Office of Special Education
Jordan Office Building
Idaho State Department
  of Education
650 West State
Boise, ID 83720
(208) 334-3940

Illinois
Educational Innovation/Support
  Section N-242
Illinois State Board of Education
100 North First Street
Springfield, IL 62777
(217) 782-2826

Indiana
Gifted/Talented Education
Indiana Department of Public
  Instruction
299 State House
Indianapolis, IN 46204
(317) 269-9663

Iowa
Gifted Education
Iowa Department of Public
  Instruction
Grimes State Office Buildng
Des Moines, IA 50319-0146
(515) 281-3198

Kansas
Gifted Education Program
Kansas State Department
  of Education
120 E. 10th
Topeka, KS 66612
(913) 296-3743

Kentucky
Gifted/Talented Education
Kentucky Department of Education
1831 Capitol Plaza Tower
Frankfort, KY 40601
(502) 564-2672

Louisiana
Gifted and Talented Programs
Louisiana Department of
 Education
P.O. Box 94604
Baton Rouge, LA 70804-9064
(504) 342-3635

Maine
Gifted and Talented Programs
Maine Department of Educational
 Services
State House Station #23
Augusta, ME 04333
(207) 289-5952

Maryland
Learning Improvement Section
Maryland State Department of
 Education
200 W. Baltimore St.
Baltimore, MD 21201
(301) 333-2357

Massachusetts
Office of Gifted and Talented
Bureau of Curriculum Services
Massachusetts Department of
 Education
1385 Hancock Street
Quincy, MA 02169
(617) 784-6717

Michigan
Programs for Gifted and Talented
Michigan Department of Education
P.O. Box 30008
Lansing, MI 48909
(517) 373-3279

Minnesota
Gifted Education
Minnesota State Department of
 Education
641 Capitol Square
St. Paul, MN 55101
(612) 296-4072

Mississippi
Programs for Gifted and Talented
Bureau of Special Services
Mississippi Department of
 Education
P.O. Box 771
Jackson, MS 39205-0771
(601) 359-3490

Missouri
Gifted Education Programs
Missouri State Department
 of Elementary and Secondary
 Education
P.O. Box 480
100 East Capitol
Jefferson City, MO 65102
(314) 751-2453

Montana
Gifted and Talented Programs
Montana Office of Public
 Instruction
Helena, MT 59620
(406) 444-4422

Nebraska
Program for the Gifted
Nebraska State Department of
  Education
P.O. Box 94987
300 Centennial Mall South
Lincoln, NE 68509
(402) 471-4337

Nevada
Special Education Programs
Nevada Department of Education
400 West King Street
Carson City, NV 89710
(702) 885-3140

New Hampshire
Office of Special Education
New Hampshire Department of
  Education
State Office Park South
101 Pleasant Street
Concord, NH 03301
(603) 271-3452

New Jersey
Division of General Academic
  Education
New Jersey Department of
  Education
225 West State Street, CN 500
Trenton, NJ 08625-0500
(609) 633-7180

New Mexico
Special Education
New Mexico State Department of
  Education
Education Building
Santa Fe, NM 87501-2786
(505) 827-6541

New York
Gifted Education
New York State Department of
  Education
Room 314-B EB
Albany, NY 12234
(518) 474-5966

North Carolina
Academically Gifted Programs
Division for Exceptional Children
North Carolina State Department
  of Public Instruction
Raleigh, NC 27611
(919) 733-3004

North Dakota
Special Education
North Dakota Department of
  Public Instruction
State Capitol
Bismarck, ND 58505
(701) 224-2277

Ohio
Programs for Gifted
Division of Special Education
933 High Street
Worthington, OH 43085
(614) 466-2650

Oklahoma
Gifted/Talented Section
Oklahoma State Department of
  Education
2500 N. Lincoln Blvd.
Oklahoma City, OK 73105
(405) 521-4287

Oregon
Gifted/Talented Program
Oregon State Department of
  Education
700 Pringle Parkway SE
Salem, OR 97219
(503) 378-4765

Pennsylvania
Bureau of Special Education
Pennsylvania Department of
  Education
333 Market Street
Harrisburg, PA 17126-0333
(717) 783-6913

Rhode Island
Gifted/Talented Education
Department of Elementary/
  Secondary Education
22 Hayes Street
Providence, RI 02908
(401) 227-6523

South Carolina
Programs for the Gifted
802 Rutledge Buildng
1429 Senate Street
Columbia, SC 29201
(803) 734-8385

South Dakota
Special Education Section
Kneip Building
South Dakota Department of
  Education
700 N. Illinois
Pierre, SD 57501
(605) 773-3678

Tennessee
Gifted/Talented Programs and
  Services
132-A Cordell Hull Building
Nashville, TN 37219
(615) 741-0662

Texas
Gifted/Talented Education
Texas Education Agency
1701 Congress Avenue
Austin, TX 78701
(512) 463-9455

Utah
Gifted Programs
Utah State Office of Education
250 E. 5th, South
Salt Lake City, UT 84111
(801) 533-5572

Vermont
Arts/Gifted Program
Vermont State Department of
  Education
Montpelier, VT 05602
(802) 828-3111, ext. 33

Virginia
Gifted Education Programs
Virginia Department of Education
P.O. Box 6Q
Richmond, VA 23216-2060
(804) 255-2070

Washington
Programs for the Gifted
Superintendent of Public
  Instruction
Old Capitol Building FG-11
Olympia, WA 98504
(206) 753-2858

West Virginia
Programs for the Gifted
West Virginia Department of
  Education
357 B, Capitol Complex
Charleston, WV 25305
(304) 348-2696

Wisconsin
School Improvement Office
P.O. Box 7841
125 S. Webster
Madison, WI 53707
(608) 267-2063

Wyoming
Gifted/Talented Programs
Wyoming Department of
  Education
Hathaway Building
Cheyenne, WY 82002
(307) 777-6226

ABOUT THE AUTHORS

Joan Franklin Smutny is director of the Center for Gifted at the National College of Education in Evanston, Illinois.

Rita Haynes Blocksam is a consultant in gifted education in Newburgh, Indiana.